Toward the Cross

Heart-Shaping Lessons for Lent and Easter

Taylor Mills

With Gary Thompson and Michelle Morris

Abingdon Press
Nashville

TOWARD THE CROSS:
HEART-SHAPING LESSONS FOR LENT AND EASTER

Excerpted from *Adult Bible Studies* and *Daily Bible Studies*, Spring 2019.
Copyright © 2018 by Cokesbury.
TOWARD THE CROSS copyright © 2022 by Abingdon Press.

Scripture quotations unless noted otherwise are taken from the Common English Bible, copyright © 2011. Used by permission. All rights reserved.

Scripture quotations noted KJV taken from The Authorized (King James) Version. Rights in the Authorized Version in the United Kingdom are vested in the Crown. Reproduced by permission of the Crown's patentee, Cambridge University Press.

Scripture quotations noted NASB taken from the New American Standard Bible® (NASB), Copyright © 1960, 1962, 1963, 1968, 1971, 1972, 1973, 1975, 1977, 1995 by The Lockman Foundation. Used by permission. www.Lockman.org

Scripture quotations noted NRSV taken from the New Revised Standard Version Bible (NRSV), copyright © 1989 National Council of the Churches of Christ in the United States of America. Used by permission. All rights reserved worldwide. http://nrsvbibles.org/

Scriptures noted NIV taken from the Holy Bible, New International Version®, NIV®. Copyright © 1973, 1978, 1984, 2011 by Biblica, Inc.™ Used by permission of Zondervan. All rights reserved worldwide. www.zondervan.com The "NIV" and "New International Version" are trademarks registered in the United States Patent and Trademark Office by Biblica, Inc.™

All web addresses were correct and operational at the time of publication.

Print Version ISBN: 9781791028947

ePub ISBN: 9781791028954

CONTENTS

Introduction 1

Ash Wednesday 3

1. A Humble Heart 11
   The First Sunday in Lent
   Daily Readings

2. A Committed Heart 32
   The Second Sunday in Lent
   Daily Readings

3. A Gracious Heart 53
   The Third Sunday in Lent
   Daily Readings

4. A Heart for Seekers 74
   The Fourth Sunday in Lent
   Daily Readings

5. A Purposeful Heart 96
The Fifth Sunday in Lent
Daily Readings

6. A Heart of Extravagant Love 118
The Sixth Sunday in Lent
Daily Readings

7. A Joyful Heart 139
Easter
Easter Monday

INTRODUCTION

Want to know what's important, what should have priority in your life, what should most concern you? Want to know what thoughts should race around most frequently in your head, what issues should keep you awake at night, what problems you should tackle first? Want to know what will make your life infinitely better and more successful?

It's not difficult to discern, at least according to our culture. Press and news media, music and radio, digital platforms, film and television, books, sports, art, celebrities, businesses and their products—all claim to know what's best and most important for us.

But when the screens go blank, when the sounds are muted, when you yank your hand away from the world's tight grasp and place it on your heart, whose voice do you hear? What do you declare is most important? It's a question we as followers of Christ must ask and answer not once, but every day. When we relinquish that power, the world is all too eager to assume it, to take it from us. Every day, we must reclaim that right and responsibility. We must decide each day that our thoughts, words, and actions will reflect the presence of Christ in our lives.

1

It's rarely an easy choice. That's why Jesus told would-be followers to count the cost. If we want easy, Jesus said, the world has plenty to offer. But none of it compares to the life we find in him. Our commitment to Christ must be more important than anything else. It must be our highest priority. When it is, we begin to develop the proper perspective on ourselves, others, and things. We learn to let go of the past, of our guilt, of things that weigh us down. And we learn to cling tightly to Christ, whose presence and power enable us to declare, "No. This is what's important." And with that declaration, with that power and presence in our lives, we can move courageously onto a path we may not understand and into a future we cannot predict.

This book, designed for use during Lent and through Easter, challenges us to answer questions that lie at the heart of discipleship: Is following Jesus the most important thing to you? Is it your priority? When we follow Jesus, how does it change the way we think, speak, and act?

"Those who find their lives will lose them," Jesus said, "and those who lose their lives because of me will find them" (Matthew 10:39).

ASH WEDNESDAY
Matthew 10:34-39

Sometimes Jesus' sayings include radical material. Luke's version of Matthew 10:34-39 is even more shocking than Matthew's account. Luke reports Jesus saying, "Whoever comes to me and doesn't hate father and mother, spouse and children, and brothers and sisters—yes, even one's own life—cannot be my disciple." He goes on to insist, "Whoever doesn't carry their own cross and follow me cannot be my disciple" (Luke 14:26-27).

Jesus sometimes used hyperbole to drive home his point. Surely, Jesus did not mean we all have to hate our own families to be his disciple. On the other hand, we should recognize that disciples of Jesus may at times find themselves in conflict with those they love.

It's interesting to note that Jesus actually talked more about our cross than he talked of his. We rarely think about this. We would much rather talk about how Jesus died on the cross of Calvary for our sins than to talk about how we should be taking up our cross.

Dietrich Bonhoeffer (1906-1945) was a German pastor who was known for his vocal resistance to Adolf Hitler and his Nazi regime. He was arrested in April 1943, imprisoned, and eventually transferred to a Nazi concentration camp. He was executed by hanging on April 9, 1945, only two weeks before his camp was liberated by American soldiers.

Bonhoeffer wrote a number of books worth reading. In *The Cost of Discipleship*, first published in 1937 when Hitler was gaining power in Germany, Bonhoeffer centered his thoughts on an exposition of the Sermon on the Mount. He sought to explain what it means to be a disciple of Jesus Christ.

Bonhoeffer made a distinction between "costly" and "cheap" grace. He explained that cheap grace is forgiveness without repentance; it is grace without discipleship. Bonhoeffer had watched too many Christians who claimed God's gift of salvation but who were unwilling to take a stand against the evil he saw rising up around him.

Bonhoeffer explained how as Christianity spread around the world, the church became increasingly secularized. The result was that the gospel was cheapened and only a few in the monastic movement tended to take discipleship seriously.

Jesus never proposed an ascetic life for its own sake but insisted upon a life of committed discipleship. Our emphasis on the cross of Christ should never deflect us from an equal emphasis on our own cross.

Dear God, help me recognize the cost of discipleship. Amen.

THURSDAY

John 12:20-26

I was born, raised, and have lived most of my life in Mississippi. Like any other place, I suppose, it has had some wonderful people and some not so wonderful. One of my greatest heroes was a woman by the name of Oseola McCarty. Mrs. McCarty was no Bible scholar, but she understood at a deep level what Jesus was talking about in these verses from John 12—perhaps better than most Bible scholars. And unlike too many of us, she practiced what she preached.

For many years this humble washerwoman of very limited means earned 50 cents per load of laundry she washed for the well-to-do families in Hattiesburg, Mississippi. She used a pot and washboard rather than an electric washing machine.

Mrs. McCarty dropped out of school when she was in the sixth grade to take care of a sick family member. She never married nor had children of her own. Though she never made much money, she lived very simply, saved a little bit each week, then put it in a savings account at the local bank.

By the time she finally had to retire in 1994 because of debilitating arthritis, she had managed to save $250,000. This was more than she felt she needed to continue her frugal lifestyle, so she decided to donate $150,000 to the University of Southern Mississippi there in Hattiesburg to help black students have the opportunity for an education she never had.

This poor washerwoman recognized the importance of

food, clothing, and shelter. Perhaps better than most. However, she also recognized that owning more and more stuff did not bring more and more happiness. She understood that success in life is not measured by the size of your house, the cost of your car, nor the designer label on your clothes.

Too many Christians in our wealthy culture have either forgotten or simply ignored the story of Zacchaeus. This rich tax collector's attitude toward money and material goods was radically changed when he met Jesus. While the rich young ruler refused to share his wealth, Zacchaeus responded to Jesus, "Look, Lord, I give half of my possessions to the poor. And if I have cheated anyone, I repay them four times as much" (Luke 19:8b).

Jesus' call to discipleship is a call to die to self and live for others. It means to live in this world, but with a keen awareness that it is only temporal while God's kingdom is eternal. Jesus said, "Stop collecting treasures for your own benefit on earth, where moth and rust eat them and where thieves break in and steal them. Instead, collect treasures for yourselves in heaven. . . . Where your treasure is, there your heart will be also" (Matthew 6:19-21).

Dear God, teach me to value the things of your kingdom. Amen.

FRIDAY

Philippians 3:7-16

Before I was a pastor, I worked in the insurance business. I started my sales career earlier while I was in college selling dictionaries door-to-door in the summer. During that time, I learned several traditional "secrets of success." Four of them are passion, persistence, find a need and fill it, and setting personal goals.

Passion is an important key to success in life. As a rule the people who achieve the most in life are passionate about what they are doing. Their passion breeds excitement and their enthusiasm keeps them motivated when the work becomes tedious and demanding. Passion also encourages confidence.

Passion also leads to perseverance. Quitters never win and winners never quit. One of my favorite stories is about Winston Churchill's famous "Don't Ever Give Up" speech.

It's not clear who first said, "Find a need and fill it." Some attribute this famous quote to Ruth Stafford Peale, the wife of the famous pastor, motivational speaker, and author Norman Vincent Peale. Robert Schuller, a protégé of Norman Vincent Peale often added, "Find a hurt and heal it."

Of course, most everyone knows that setting goals is important in achieving success. It's hard to hit a target that you can't see. Having a clear vision of what you want to accomplish is vital.

The apostle Paul apparently understood all these keys to

success. More than once he compared his life to one running a race, and he was passionate about not only finishing, but also winning. If anyone knew about perseverance it was Paul. He persevered despite horrible persecution. To the church at Corinth he wrote, "We did this with our great endurance through problems, disasters, and stressful situations. We went through beatings, imprisonments, and riots. We experienced hard work, sleepless nights, and hunger" (2 Corinthians 6:4b-5).

Paul obviously believed in setting goals. His athletic metaphors suggest he understood their importance. He tells us in this text that his goal is the "resurrection of the dead." What he means by this is not totally clear, but he goes on to add "the goal I pursue is the prize of God's upward call in Christ Jesus" (verse 14).

What is clear about the apostle's goals is that he sought to be an obedient disciple of Jesus Christ. This was most important. He served Christ by serving others. He found a need that all people share, and he passionately dedicated his life to filling that need at all cost.

Dear God, fill my heart with your passion and help me identify the goals you have for my life. Amen.

SATURDAY

Luke 14:15-24

I love the old story about a first-grade teacher who gave her class an interesting assignment. Each student was to bring something to school the next day that would represent his or her religion.

The next morning, the teacher first called on Jacob to tell about the item he brought. He stood up and explained, "I am Jewish, and this is the Star of David, a symbol of my religion." Mary was next. She stood up and said, "I am Catholic, and this rosary is a symbol of my religion." The teacher then called on Jimmy. Rather hesitantly, he held up a casserole dish as he said, "I am a Methodist."

Of course, Methodists are not the only Christians who like to get together and eat. Christians have been doing that since the time of Jesus. In fact, Jesus often suggested that the kingdom of God is something like a party.

Several years ago, a survey was conducted during a mission conference. People were asked, What image do you have in mind when you present the gospel of Jesus Christ to someone? Do you see it as snatching brands from the burning fire or as inviting people to a feast? Most of the pastors indicated that they thought of it more as snatching people from a burning fire. The missionaries tended to see it more as inviting people to a feast.

I grew up attending a church where the vast majority of

members and pastors see their mission as "snatching brands from the burning fire." However, as I began to read and study the Bible more and more, paying particular attention to the "red letters" (the words of Jesus, as printed in some Bibles), I came increasingly to see the mission of the church in a different way.

While Jesus did talk about punishment for sins, he emphasized a positive message. God will be the final judge, but Jesus spent most of his time healing the broken and pointing people to ways of living a more fruitful and meaningful life here on earth.

In Matthew 11, we are told that when John the Baptizer heard about the amazing things that Jesus was doing, he sent his disciples to ask the Lord a question: "Are you the one who is to come, or should we look for another?" (Matthew 11:3).

Jesus surely answered the question in a way that would explain how he understood his own ministry: "*Those who were blind are able to see.* Those who were crippled are walking. People with skin diseases are cleansed. Those *who were deaf now hear. Those who were dead are raised up. The poor have good news proclaimed to them*" (Matthew 11:5-6). He could have said that many are being invited to God's party.

Dear God, thank you for inviting me to your party. Amen.

1

A HUMBLE HEART

The First Sunday in Lent

Luke 14:7-14

Out of the mouths of babes!

The children came from Sunday school where they had just heard the story from Luke 14:7-14. Jesus' instructions on hospitality were fresh on their minds: "When you host a lunch or dinner, don't invite your friends, your brothers and sisters, your relatives, or rich neighbors" (Luke 14:12).

Now it was time for the congregational announcements in the worship service. "After church today, we hope you will all come to our churchwide potluck lunch in the fellowship hall," said the pastor. "And it's not too late to invite a friend, a family member, or a neighbor."

Up went a little hand. "Yes?" the pastor said, expecting the boy to say something that everyone would find adorable.

"Jesus said not to invite those folks," came the voice, loud enough for everyone to hear. Awkward!

This text from Matthew leads us to explore Jesus' lessons on humility and hospitality at the table—and even beyond the table.

With some divine inspiration and creativity, we can discover ways to be authentically humble and radically hospitable in our churches and in every place. After all, hasn't God shown us ultimate hospitality by accepting us as sons and daughters?

As a Guest

It seems like every small town in America has one: a group of friends who gather for breakfast early every morning at a diner or a fast-food restaurant. After they finish their eggs and hash browns, they serve up a good portion of local news and opinion, some of it perhaps a little salty at times.

The breakfast group might not realize it, but their informal ritual is much like the ancient Greek symposium, an after-dinner time when men would tell epic stories, impart wisdom, or match wits. Symposiums were still fairly common in Jesus' time, and the meal described in Luke 14 might have been one.

A symposium was usually an enjoyable event. But on this occasion, there was already tension in the air as Jesus arrived. Jesus' host was a Pharisee leader (Luke 14:1), and the Pharisees had already begun grumbling against Jesus.

On his way to this meal, Jesus had already healed a man

with "an abnormal swelling of the body" (verse 2; "dropsy" in some older translations). Some of the Pharisees didn't like the fact that Jesus healed the man on the sabbath, so Luke tells us that the leaders of the Pharisees "were watching him closely" (verse 1).

And Jesus watched them right back. As the guests took their seats at the table, he "noticed how the guests sought out the best seats at the table" (verse 7). Jesus saw this as a teachable moment. He didn't wait until after the meal. He didn't even wait for everyone to be seated. Right at the start, he taught them lessons in humility and hospitality. He told the guests to always take their seat in the least important place rather than in the seat of honor. "Then you will be honored in the presence of all your fellow guests" (verse 10).

Awkward!

What did the host think of all this? Did he immediately regret inviting Jesus? And what about the one who was sitting in the seat of honor when Jesus made these remarks? Was there a shuffling of seats after Jesus gave this lesson in humility?

There was no mistaking Jesus' words. He called the guests out for seeking to honor themselves.

Was this a new teaching? Not necessarily. The Pharisees probably knew the proverb that says, "Don't exalt yourself in the presence of the king, or stand in the place of important people, because it is better that he say to you, 'Come up here,' than to be demoted before a ruler" (Proverbs 25:6-7). Yet there were the guests, seeking places of honor. The way Jesus saw it, you were not to seize honor for yourself.

13

Honor was to be bestowed by others, and ultimate honor was God's to give. Just as Peter wrote in his first letter, "Humble yourselves under God's power so that he may raise you up in the last day" (1 Peter 5:6). Readers of Matthew's Gospel remember Jesus saying, "All who lift themselves up will be brought low. But all who make themselves low will be lifted up" (Matthew 23:12).

And who could ever forget that conversation on the way to Jerusalem when the mother of James and John bowed before Jesus to implore him, "Say that these two sons of mine will sit, one on your right hand and one on your left, in your kingdom" (Matthew 20:21)? What a contrast with Luke 14:7-11.

It is Jesus' practical example to us of how to exercise humility at a meal. And if the table fellowship is a microcosm of our larger life together, how do Jesus' teachings here inform how we exercise humility at the table and in every place?

Where can you apply Jesus' teaching on humility in the coming days?

As a Host

There's a great episode of *The Andy Griffith Show* when Otis has to stay at the house with Aunt Bee because the jail is at capacity.[1] Aunt Bee is in her kitchen with two friends, baking cakes for the church supper. She is mortified to think that her respectable guests might encounter uncouth and drunk Otis in her house. So Aunt Bee decides to reform Otis during his stay in her "jail." She will straighten him out through her own work program of household chores.

At first, Otis didn't like it at all. But by the end of the episode, he has dried out and cleaned up. It may have taken Aunt Bee some time to open her home and heart to him, but she eventually saw him as worthy of hospitality.

Hospitality was the basis of the second part of Jesus' teaching in this text. He was still at the dining event with his Pharisee host and his guests. They had just gotten a lesson in humility from Jesus.

Now Jesus shifted his focus from the guests to the host: "When you host a lunch or dinner, don't invite your friends, your brothers and sisters, your relatives, or rich neighbors. . . . Instead, when you give a banquet, invite the poor, crippled, lame, and blind" (Luke 14:12, 13). Just as the guests were to seek the lowest place, the host was to seek guests with low social standing, people who would probably not be able to return the favor. Was this a new teaching? It was certainly radical!

For example, the Pharisees at this meal must have been familiar with God's law in Leviticus that prohibited people who were physically imperfect from entering parts of the holy sanctuary and making an offering to God (Leviticus 21:17-23).

In the Dead Sea Scrolls, scholars found a document with the invitation list for a great banquet at the end of human history. Welcome were "all the wise men of the congregation, the learned and the intelligent, men whose way is perfect and men of ability . . . the men of renown."

Who was not invited? "No man smitten in his flesh, or paralyzed in his feet or hands, or lame, or blind, or deaf, or dumb, or smitten in his flesh with a visible blemish; no old and

15

tottery man unable to stay still in the midst of the congregation."

When Patrick J. Willson read this list to a class in his church, an octogenarian laughed and declared, "Preacher, you know that business about tottery old men who can't stay still in the middle of church? They're saying they don't want folks with weak bladders!"[2]

So when Jesus told his host to invite the "poor, crippled, lame, and blind," he was teaching an important lesson on hospitality. As he said in the previous chapter, "Those who are last will be first and those who are first will be last" (Luke 13:30). He gave honor and respect to those who were considered unworthy and taught those around him to do the same.

The poor, crippled, lame, and blind were generally not afforded the same privileges as the wealthy and able-bodied. One commentator has observed that "in terms of status, these people are clearly peasants or worse. . . . Yet they are God's chosen guests. God would have the wealthy, elite members of the Lukan church invite them to full membership and equal status with them."[3]

I doubt any of us object to Jesus' teaching on whom to invite to a dinner party. But let's be honest. How many of us follow it?

I confess that I haven't gone out and intentionally invited the poor, crippled, lame, and blind to my house for a meal, and I lived in church-owned parsonages for many years! I like to think I wouldn't turn anyone away, but Jesus wasn't talking about that. He said to go out and invite them.

Shouldn't the same go for the meals we host in our churches? Jesus didn't just tell us to welcome everyone who may come. He said to actually go out and invite those who are socially ignored or outcast. The duty falls to Christians to go out of their way to make the invitation.

We good church folks may not like being implicated in Jesus' words, and I doubt the Pharisees did either. But neither should we try to exonerate ourselves or relativize Jesus' clear teaching. Our best response is to confess that we do not measure up, to ask the Lord for help to do better, and to go and do as he taught us.

A few years ago, I was the pastor of a city church when I heard about a ministry that was taking free meals to people who lived in the woods and under the bridges of our city. Most days, the servers would eat together with the guests and the guests would help the servers clean up. In these ways, they blended the roles of caregiver and care recipient.

The director of the ministry was a clergy colleague of mine, so we struck up a conversation about how we might collaborate. At that time, her office was her car and the ministry's base of operations was a storage unit. But our church could provide her with a proper office and a location closer to the downtown population she wanted to reach. So we did.

Today the church and the table ministry have a rich, symbiotic relationship as they exhibit Jesus' humility and hospitality together.

Where might we manifest humble hospitality at the table? Who is missing from the table and why?

As a People

Jesus' mealtime lessons in humility and hospitality were more than just etiquette. Jesus re-ordered priorities. He gave us a peek at the kingdom of God where "all who lift themselves up will be brought low, and those who make themselves low will be lifted up" (Luke 14:11).

These lessons were expressed around the table, but they weren't limited to the table. Jesus expressed the same humility and hospitality in his life, death, and resurrection.

The early Christians put it in beautiful verse: "When he found himself in the form of a human, he humbled himself by becoming obedient to the point of death, even death on a cross" (Philippians 2:7-8).

Jesus humbly put God's will before his own that we might have access to God through him. That was an ultimate act of hospitality. God showed us the greatest hospitality by giving us eternal life. Even us!

Many know that John Wesley wrote that on May 24, 1738, he felt his heart "strangely warmed." But the next sentence is just as important. He went on to explain, "I felt I did trust in Christ, Christ alone for salvation; and an assurance was given me that He had taken away my sins, even mine."

I've always loved how he said "even mine."[4] Wesley was amazed that God would be so hospitable to accept even him. This should remind us how amazing it is that God would accept us, even us! That's hospitality!

Around the same time, John's brother Charles penned lyrics that expressed his own amazement at God's grace in accepting him:

Amazing love! How can it be
that thou, my God, shouldst die for me![5]

So, too, Jesus calls us to exhibit radical hospitality. If we
do, we "will be repaid when the just are resurrected" (Luke
14:14). When we imitate Jesus' humility and God's hospitality,
our actions have cosmic and eternal significance, not only for
ourselves but also in service to God's kingdom.

If you still have your Bible open, read verse 15. I just love
how the story ends! After Jesus had finished his remarks, an
unnamed dinner guest said to him, "Happy are those who will
feast in God's kingdom" (verse 15).

Yes! What a wonderful declaration! Perhaps it expresses how
you feel, too.

**How have you experienced God's hospitality in your own
spirit?**

*Thank you, Lord Jesus, for teaching us the virtues of humility and
hospitality. Where we have fallen short of your expectations, forgive
us, we pray. Free us to be your faithful disciples by welcoming others
the way you welcome us. Amen.*

1. From "Aunt Bee the Warden," from *The Andy Griffith Show* (Season 2), directed
   by Bob Sweeney (Paramount Television, March 12, 1962).
2. From "Sunday, August 29, 2010: Luke 14:1, 7-14," by Patrick J. Willson in
   The Christian Century, 127.17 (2010); page 20.
3. From *The Social World of Luke-Acts*, by Jerome H. Neyrey (Hendrickson
   Publishers, 2008); pages 379-380.
4. From "I Felt My Heart Strangely Warmed," by John Wesley and Percy
   Livingstone Parker in *The Journal of John Wesley* (Moody, 1951).
5. Charles Wesley, "And Can It Be that I Should Gain," *The United Methodist
   Hymnal* (Nashville: The United Methodist Publishing House, 1989); no. 363,
   stanza 1.

MONDAY

Proverbs 25:2-7

In his book on the life of Benjamin Franklin, Carl Van Doren relates an incident that happened when Franklin once went to visit the noted Puritan minister Cotton Mather. He quotes the famous writer, scientist, and signer of the Declaration of Independence and our nation's Constitution:

"He received me in his library and, on my taking leave, showed me a shorter way out of the house through a narrow passage, which was crossed by a beam overhead. We were still talking as I withdrew, he accompanying me behind, when he said hastily; 'Stoop, stoop!' I did not understand him, till I felt my head hit against the beam. He was a man that never missed an occasion of giving instruction, and upon this he said to me: 'You are young, and have the world before you; stoop as you go through it, and you will miss many hard thumps."[1]

Today's text deals with the traditional social order during the writer's time and place. We can hardly read verses 6-7 without recalling the words of Jesus as recorded in Luke 14:8-11. The Book of Proverbs has a great deal to say about pride and humility. For example, Proverbs 16:18-19 says, "Pride comes before disaster, and arrogance before a fall. Better to be humble with the needy than to divide plunder with the proud." Another verse on pride is found in Proverbs 29:23, where the author insisted, "Pride lays people low, but those of humble spirit gain honor."

A prideful person may fool enough people to rise to a position of power and prestige for a time, but he or she is likely to be found out eventually. Pride prevents people from growing in mind and spirit. They think they know everything already. Those who think they are better than others are less likely to recognize their own weaknesses and failures and may not even seek to improve. Of course, the greatest danger is to be so prideful that we don't recognize our own need for God.

Dear God, teach me how to have a healthy opinion of myself. Amen.

1. From *Benjamin Franklin,* by Carl Van Doren (New York: Viking Press, 1938); pages 43-44.

TUESDAY

James 2:1-7

I immediately thought of this Scripture passage recently when I read about a church on the Sunday its new pastor was to be introduced. Some of the leaders of the church were sitting up front preparing to start the morning worship service when a shabbily dressed homeless man walked into the sanctuary. He made his way to a pew near the front of the room, but an usher quietly asked him to move to the back row.

After the service started, one of the leaders got up to introduce their new pastor. Most of the congregation was quite surprised when the "homeless" man made his way up front. There he began to describe his experience. Out of the several hundred people present, only a couple of people had even spoken to him. He had been made to feel quite unwelcome.

The author of the Book of James could not have made it clearer. If there is any favoritism to be shown in God's kingdom, it is the poor who should get preferential treatment. Unfortunately, this is not always the case in the church.

Jesus had a great deal to say about the poor. In fact, when he preached his first sermon at his home synagogue in Nazareth, he read his text from the prophet Isaiah: "*The Spirit of the Lord is upon me, because the Lord has anointed me. He has sent me to preach good news to the poor, to proclaim release to the prisoners and recovery of sight to the blind, to liberate the oppressed, and to proclaim the year of the Lord's favor*" (Luke 4:18-19).

Luke's version of the Beatitudes begins, "Happy are you who are poor, because God's kingdom is yours. Happy are you who hunger now, because you will be satisfied. Happy are you who weep now, because you will laugh" (Luke 6:20-21). Jesus even insisted that we will ultimately be judged by how we treat the poor, not by what doctrines we hold. The Gospel writer spells this out in Matthew 25:31-46.

So who are the sheep who will inherit the Kingdom? Jesus proclaimed they are the ones who feed the hungry, give drink to the thirsty, give clothes to the naked, take care of the sick, and visit those in prison. In other words, they are the ones who care for the poor and the disenfranchised.

Dear God, fill my heart with your love for the poor and the vulnerable of this world. Amen.

WEDNESDAY

Matthew 5:43-48

People in our country have for many years been embroiled in a huge debate. Some people want to keep refugees who claim to be fleeing persecution out of our country. Many Christians support these efforts, while others point to verses like the ones in today's Scripture.

I can understand a person's desire to keep their family as safe as possible. I also acknowledge that determining what Jesus' commandment to love our enemies means in practice can be difficult and we may have honest disagreements about how we put that instruction into practice.

However, what continues to trouble me about this debate is the hateful language and uncaring attitudes I repeatedly see among many people who identify themselves as Christians. The people to whom Jesus was speaking in his Sermon on the Mount were no doubt familiar with his quote from Leviticus 19:18: "You must not take revenge nor hold a grudge against any of your people; instead, you must love your neighbor as yourself; I am the LORD." Note that the neighbor referred to in this verse was "any of your people." That is to say, it was their Jewish neighbor they were to love.

This is the key difference between the teachings of Jesus and the common Jewish traditions and beliefs of that time. Jesus expanded the meaning of neighbor. In Luke 10, we learn about a legal expert who sought to test Jesus when he asked what he had to do to gain eternal life. Jesus put the question back to him: "What is written in the Law? How do you interpret it?" (Luke 10:26). The man responded, *"You must love the Lord your God with all your heart, with all your being, with all your strength, and with all your mind, and love your neighbor as yourself"* (Luke 10:27).

This answer was actually no surprise. Every religious Jew knows the Shema, a centerpiece of the morning and evening Jewish prayer service, whose opening lines are taken from Deuteronomy 6:5. The legal expert was simply quoting this verse. He also quoted the well-known passage from Leviticus 19:18.

After Jesus affirmed his answer, the man questioned the Lord: "And who is my neighbor?" (Luke 10:29). To this, Jesus responded by relating the story of the good Samaritan. By telling this story, he was insisting that God wants us to see every human being as a neighbor who is to be loved. Today's text makes this even more explicit and drives home the point that this even includes our enemies.

Dear God, transform my heart and fill me with your love for all people. Amen.

THURSDAY

Ephesians 4:1-7

In yesterday's reading, we were reminded of just how divided we are in this country. We have even named the sections that tend to lean to the right or to the left. We call them red and blue states. Of course, there is nothing new with this. These differences continue to linger long after a great civil war was fought over similar issues. Even more distressing for me is that these same divisions pry their way into the life of the church. Christians are not immune to these terrible divisions.

Of course, there is nothing new about this, either. From the earliest times, the church found itself embroiled in dispute. The author of Ephesians gave practical advice about how a Christian should live out his or her faith. He began with a discussion about Christian unity. He seemed to understand that the only person we can actually change is ourselves. The secret to unity is simple. Each of us should conduct ourselves "with all humility, gentleness, and patience" and "accept each other with love" (Ephesians 4:2).

Whether the arguments that divide us today are political or theological, it seems that everyone is totally convinced they are right. Often, perhaps most of the time, humility, gentleness, and patience are missing from the debates. We talk past one another without even hearing, much less giving careful consideration, to what the other person is saying. Instead of listening intently to the other person, our minds are busy formulating our rebuttal.

We seldom consider that we might actually be wrong about anything.

Matthew 5:5 records the third Beatitude, famously translated in the King James Version: "Blessed are the meek; for they shall inherit the earth." The Common English Bible reads, "Happy are people who are humble." Perhaps the translation closest to the original Greek is "Blessed are the gentle," as rendered by the New American Standard Version.

A gentle horse is one that allows the rider to take control. The horse goes where and when the rider wills and at the speed the rider wishes. Rather than resisting, the horse submits. When we submit to the will of God, as instructed by Christ, we will act as Paul encouraged us. We will indeed conduct ourselves with all humility, gentleness, and patience. Even more importantly, we will accept one another with love and accept our differences.

In today's passage, Paul reminds us that there is diversity in our unity. Unity is not uniformity. We are all different, with different God-given gifts. It takes all kinds to make a world, and it takes all kinds to make the kingdom of God. We should be thankful that not everyone thinks alike or is just like us.

Dear God, teach us to accept one another with love. Amen.

| **FRIDAY** |

Luke 14:1-6

This marks the third time Luke reports that Jesus healed someone on the sabbath. The other accounts give us a bit more information from which we can draw conclusions.

The first account is found in Luke 6:6. There we are told that Jesus entered a synagogue to teach. The legal experts and Pharisees present were watching Jesus carefully, just as in today's text from Luke 14. However, in Chapter 6, Luke tells us why they were doing so. They were watching to see if he would break the Law by healing someone because "they were looking for a reason to bring charges against him" (Luke 6:7). A man with a withered hand was brought to him. Even though Jesus knew what the lawyers and Pharisees were up to, he healed the man immediately. When the religious leaders saw that the man's hand was healthy, "They were furious and began talking with each other about what to do to Jesus" (6:11).

Luke's second account of Jesus healing on the sabbath is found in Luke 13:10-17. Again, Jesus was in a synagogue when he healed a woman "who had been disabled by a spirit for eighteen years" (13:11). The synagogue leader criticized Jesus for doing this on the sabbath. He apparently felt that if she had been in this condition for 18 years, she could certainly have waited one more day. Jesus defended himself: "Hypocrites! Don't each of you on the Sabbath untie your ox or donkey from its stall and lead it out to get a drink?" (13:15).

Luke 6:1-6 records an occasion when Jesus was walking through a wheat field on the sabbath with his disciples, who were picking grains of wheat and eating them. Some Pharisees saw them and questioned Jesus: "Why are you breaking the Sabbath law?" (6:2). Jesus ended his defense with the statement, "The Human One [or "Son of Man"] is Lord of the Sabbath" (6:5). Mark's Gospel precedes this statement with, "The Sabbath was created for humans; humans weren't created for the Sabbath" (Mark 2:27).

Jesus believed that the laws were made for the benefit of humankind and should be applied in a way that was most beneficial for humankind. God doesn't sit around making up rules that make it difficult for us.

Stop signs aren't placed on our roads as obstacles for our travels. They are there for our protection. God's laws should never be ignored but should always be applied with great compassion and understanding. We need to remember this when political and theological debates threaten the harmony and unity in our churches.

Dear God, teach me to apply your laws with the same compassion and understanding as did Jesus. Amen.

SATURDAY

Mark 1:16-20; Luke 14:25-33

One day, a man came to Jesus and asked, "Good Teacher, what must I do to obtain eternal life?" (Mark 10:17). Jesus reminded him of the commandments. After the man insisted that he had always kept these commandments, Jesus said, "You are lacking one thing. Go, sell what you own, and give the money to the poor. Then you will have treasure in heaven. And come, follow me." The man didn't like this answer so he "went away saddened, because he had many possessions" (verses 21-22).

I have always found it interesting that Jesus didn't call this man back and try to renegotiate the deal. "Oh," Jesus might have said, "perhaps if you just gave 10 percent of what you own, that would be sufficient for now. Then later you might be ready to do more." Jesus never pulled punches. He never watered down the gospel. He never offered cheap grace.

Today's text records Jesus once again insisting on a total commitment. "Whoever doesn't carry their own cross and follow me cannot be my disciple" (Luke 14:27). He emphasized the importance of counting the cost before we commit ourselves to him. He wanted everyone to know up front that being his disciple could be costly. It costs some their very lives.

I made my public profession of faith and joined a church when I was a young child. I was told by the pastor that all I had to do was invite Jesus into my heart. There was absolutely no talk

30

about repentance and certainly none about costly discipleship. Not all preachers present the gospel the way Jesus did, calling men and women to repentance and Christian discipleship.

When people do talk about carrying their cross, they are usually talking about some painful chronic illness or difficulty they have to face on a regular basis. It is an involuntary curse. This is not what Jesus was talking about. To take up our cross and follow Jesus means to voluntarily submit ourselves to his lordship and to do whatever God calls us to do, no matter the cost.

From time to time I listen to preachers on television. They often talk about the benefits of being a Christian. There is no conflict between their message and the material values of middle-class Americans. This kind of message was not the one Jesus proclaimed, which calls people to a radical rejection of materialism. "None of you who are unwilling to give up all of your possessions can be my disciple," Jesus said (Luke 14:33).

Dear God, transform my heart, and change my priorities, values, and pursuits. Amen.

2

A COMMITTED HEART

The Second Sunday in Lent

Mark 1:16-20; Luke 14:25-33

I just knew my parents were going to be so proud of my frugality. I had discovered a record club that would send me eight CDs for a penny! A penny! For a teenager with a new CD player, this was like finding a treasure chest.

Little did I realize what I was getting myself into. If I didn't keep sending in a special card each month, they would send me a CD I didn't order and charge me full price (somewhere north of $20). To get out of this obligation, I had to buy several CDs at full price within 12 months.

Of course, it was in the 12th month that I approached my parents with the news that I hadn't reached my purchase obligation. They were not pleased, and we worked out a solution. But I had learned my lesson: Always read the fine print, and count the cost before making a commitment.

Jesus' call to his disciples was straightforward: "Come, follow me, . . . and I'll show you how to fish for people" (Mark 1:17). But at a certain point, he looked at the large crowd and decided to teach them about counting the cost. He told them to hate their families, carry their crosses, count the costs, and give up their possessions (Luke 14:26-27, 33).

This text calls us to examine the cost of Christian discipleship. By holding our two texts in tension with one another, we will seek to understand Jesus' call to us today.

The Call

In Mark 1:16-20, Jesus' ministry was off to an immediate start. Having been baptized and tempted, he then went to Galilee and walked along the sea. There he called two sets of brothers to be his disciples: Simon and Andrew, James and John.

Mark said the disciples responded to Jesus' call "right away" and "at that very moment" (Mark 1:18, 20). But how did they give up everything to follow Jesus so quickly and easily?

I've usually heard it explained one of two ways: (1) Jesus had a mesmerizing charm that supernaturally entranced them, or (2) the brothers themselves were shining examples of dedication and devotion that we should all emulate.

If the first explanation was the case, then the disciples had little to do with their calling. But that doesn't fit because Mark made sure to tell us about all the family and fish that the men left behind.

If the second explanation was true, then Jesus had little to do with their calling. They were just fishing until something better came along. If that were the case, they might have asked for Jesus' credentials: an ordination certificate, diploma, or résumé. They might have asked if there was health insurance or a 401(k).

But, seriously, we don't know if they experienced inner angst about leaving their families, homes, or jobs to follow Jesus. Mark didn't tell us. We can only be certain that Mark focused on how they left everything to follow Jesus.

So what does it mean for us to have a Savior who calls us to follow him? Think about how amazing it is that Jesus actually desires our discipleship in the first place! He was not obligated to have followers any more than God was ever obligated to create humanity.

But Jesus called disciples. He wanted them to join him in his work. And Jesus calls us to follow him and fish for people too. Absolutely astounding!

Sometimes people assume that the ordained are the only ones with a call from God. But God has called every follower of Jesus, lay or ordained, to be in ministry.

In the tradition of The United Methodist Church, we state that "all Christians are called through their baptism to this ministry of servanthood in the world to the glory of God and for human fulfillment."[1]

We are all going about some other work when Jesus calls, whether it's the first call or the thousandth. Each of us is holding something when Jesus approaches us, be it a fishing net or a cell phone. We all have that moment to decide.

If you were one of these brothers, what would it have taken to get you to leave everything and follow Jesus? What does it take today?

The Cost

If our first text made following Jesus sound easy, our second text made it sound impossible. Luke said that "large crowds were traveling with Jesus" (Luke 14:25). Performers, politicians, and preachers tend to pay a lot of attention to crowd size, so this sounds like great news! We would love to see large crowds following Jesus today. But it seems like the size of the crowd gave Jesus concern. Perhaps he wondered if they understood how costly their commitment would be.

So Jesus warned them harshly. Three times he spoke in a formula that began with, "Whoever doesn't . . ." and ended with, "cannot be my disciple." Consider the severity of his three warnings.

In the first warning, Jesus said, "Whoever comes to me and doesn't hate father and mother, spouse and children, and brothers and sisters—yes, even one's own life—cannot be my disciple" (Luke 14:26). Hate your own family? While this kind of hyperbole was not uncommon in Semitic discourse, it probably didn't rest easy on its first hearers.[2] "Honor your father and your mother," they had learned (Exodus 20:12). Family was often the primary way they knew their identity and place in the world.

This isn't the family-friendly message that people today have come to expect from any preacher who would want to

35

grow her church. Saying, "Come to our church, and give up all your possessions" would not work well on an invitational banner in the churchyard.

But Jesus wanted his disciples to be aware of their allegiances. They should always ask themselves, Is anyone, or anything, in my life more important to me than Jesus?

Then came the second warning: "Whoever doesn't carry their own cross and follow me cannot be my disciple" (Luke 14:27). Consider what it must have sounded like in Jesus' time to hear him say such a thing.

Today people talk about their "cross to bear" in relation to physical problems, difficulties at work, or the like. But in Jesus' day and time, people thought of the cross like we think of the noose, the electric chair, or the gas chamber. The cross meant a violent death.

We should be under no illusions about what Jesus expects. Thomas à Kempis once wrote, "Jesus has always many who love His heavenly kingdom, but few who bear His cross. He has many who desire consolation, but few who care for trial. . . . Those, on the contrary, who love Him for His own sake and not for any comfort of their own, bless Him in all trial and anguish of heart as well as in the bliss of consolation . . . . What power there is in pure love for Jesus—love that is free from all self-interest and self-love!"[3]

Jesus gave two illustrations between the second and third warnings. The first illustration was about building a tower, and the second was about going to war (Luke 14:28-32). In both cases, he asked the crowd who among them wouldn't make sure to give enough money or troops to finish the task. The implicit answer was, "Well, no one, of course."

Then Jesus gave the third warning: "In the same way, none of you who are unwilling to give up all of your possessions can be my disciple" (Luke 14:33). The phrasing was a little different from the other two warnings, but the meaning was the same: Count the cost.

Readers of Luke's Gospel later encounter the "certain ruler" who asked, "What must I do to obtain eternal life?" (Luke 18:18). Jesus replied with an answer similar to his teaching here: "Sell everything you own and distribute the money to the poor" (Luke 18:22).

And in Acts, Luke went on to write about how the early church "would sell pieces of property and possessions and distribute the proceeds to everyone who needed them" (Acts 2:45) and how "none of them would say, 'This is mine!' about any of their possessions, but held everything in common" (Acts 4:32).

Family, life, and possessions. Following Jesus is costly! Being a disciple is not just one more thing to add to an already busy life. It's how we live life itself.

At one point in John's Gospel, Jesus gave a similar lesson on the cost of discipleship. John then wrote, "At this, many of his disciples turned away and no longer accompanied him" (John 6:66). I wonder if the crowd also thinned out after they heard Jesus' warnings as recorded in Luke.

How do you react to Jesus' expectations for discipleship? Do you find them off-putting or refreshing in their frankness?

The Commitment

So what's a Christian to do? In Mark, we have Jesus' call to his first disciples who instantly left everything to follow him (Mark 1:16-20). Mark almost made it sound easy. But in Luke, Jesus told the crowds that discipleship would cost them everything (Luke 14:25-33). The bar is set so high that it would seem unreachable.

Should we be more like the fishing brothers of Mark or the fickle crowds of Luke? Is it better to be all-in or to count the cost? Should we look for a happy medium between the two: committed but not too committed?

Would it be better just to slowly back away from discipleship altogether? Is that the way to show Jesus we are serious? Maybe we should just plan to come back later when we think we can do better?

Certainly not! Look at the disciples Jesus called to follow him in Mark. He called them directly, literally face to face. He didn't make a mistake. He knew their faults and limitations. He knew they didn't come off the boat ready for all that discipleship would require. And he would often find them lacking in faith or even asleep in the course of their duties (Luke 22:46)! Nevertheless, he called them and he loved them.

That's what the call to discipleship is. It's a manifestation of God's love for us. God created us to "glorify God, and to enjoy him forever," says the Westminster Catechism.[4] We Christians do this by following Jesus Christ as Lord. Sure, we must rely on the grace and power of God's Spirit to continually remake us in God's image. But God knows that.

Joseph Hart was an 18th-century minister in London who became a libertine as a young man. Hart told his biographer, "I began to sink deeper and deeper into conviction of my nature's evil, the wickedness of my life, the shallowness of my Christianity, and the blindness of my devotion."[5]

However, the week before Easter in 1757, Hart had a vision of Christ in the garden of Gethsemane that changed him forever. He experienced a renewed faith in God and rededicated himself to his Lord. Within two years, he had penned and published several hymns. Among those hymns was one that has been included in hundreds of hymnals since: "Come, Ye Sinners, Poor and Needy." It is a clarion call to Christian discipleship, especially the original lines that Hart wrote:

Come, ye sinners, poor and needy, weak and wounded, sick and sore;
Jesus ready stands to save you, full of pity, love and power.
Let not conscience make you linger, nor of fitness fondly dream;
all the fitness he requireth is to feel your need of him.
Come ye weary, heavy laden, lost and ruined by the fall;
if you tarry till you're better, you will never come at all.[6]

The call stands, regardless of our abilities. We should count the cost as Jesus teaches. But in our calculations, we should not leave out the immeasurable grace of God who counted the cost of our salvation. God found the cost to be inconceivably high but paid it anyway!

So let us come and follow Jesus. Let us put him first above all others, carry our crosses, and give of all we have to follow him.

Where do you find yourself now? In the boat hearing the call? in the crowd hearing the warnings? How do you respond?

God, help me lay aside and turn away from those things that keep me from wholeheartedly following Jesus. Remind me that disciple-ship is not just one more thing on my to-do list, but it is in fact how you call me to live. Thank you for entrusting me with your call, and give me the courage to live into it, every moment of every day. Amen.

1. From *The Book of Discipline of The United Methodist Church* (Nashville: The United Methodist Publishing House, 2016); ¶ 126.
2. From *The New Interpreter's Bible*, Volume IX (Nashville: Abingdon Press, 1995); page 292.
3. From *The Imitation of Christ*, by Thomas à Kempis (Milwaukee, Wisconsin: Bruce Publishing Company, 1940); pages 74-75.
4. From *The Westminster Shorter Catechism Ratified by the General Assembly of The Presbyterian Church in the United States at Augusta, Ga., December 4, 1861*, first edition (Presbyterian Committee of Publication, 1861); page 3.
5. From "Joseph Hart," by Thomas Wright in *The Lives of the British Hymn-Writers*, first edition (Farmcombe & Son, 1910); pages 4, 34.
6. Joseph Hart, "Come, Ye Sinners, Poor and Needy," *The United Methodist Hymnal*, no. 340, stanzas 1, 4, 3. Around 1802, Hart's original first lines were joined to a popular refrain: "I will arise and go to Jesus."

MONDAY
Mark 4:10-20

Early in my pastoral ministry, I made an important observation. I watched people join the church, sometimes with much apparent excitement about their decision. Then within a few months, or sometimes even weeks, their attendance would become increasingly sporadic until they were gone, never to return. I eventually learned this is the likely outcome unless the person gets involved in more than worship attendance on Sunday morning.

As I tried to address this problem, anytime a potential new member visited our church, I started immediately seeking ways to get that person plugged in to our church community. Waiting until they joined the church might be too late. I encouraged them to attend a Sunday school class or another small group where they could meet other people and develop personal relationships. I sought to identify their interests, their talents, and their spiritual gifts. This helped me find an appropriate job in the church for them to do in which they could find fulfillment.

Sadly, the biggest problem I ran into with this strategy was the negative response I sometimes got from established church members who felt threatened by the newcomers. They were sometimes afraid they were going to lose their position or have to give up some of their power.

I should not have been surprised by people getting excited

about joining the church and then quickly dropping out. Jesus warned us about this long ago with his parable of the sower, found here in Mark 4, in Matthew 13, and Luke 8. A farmer went out to sow seed, Jesus told the crowd. Some of the seed fell on the path, some on the rocky ground, some among thorny plants, and some among good soil. Only the seeds that fell on the good soil bore fruit.

Today's text gives us Jesus' allegorical interpretation of his parable. The seeds that fell on the path represent the skeptics who hear the gospel message but fail to accept it. The seeds that fell on the rocky ground are like those who make professions of faith and join the church but eventually fall away when something else grabs their attention or they become bored because they are not involved in anything meaningful.

The seeds that fall among thorny plants may be the most harmful to God's kingdom. These are like the ones who make a profession of faith, join the church, and stay. But rather than letting God transform their hearts and producing good fruit, they bring their worldly attitudes into the church and sometimes even manage to poison the whole atmosphere.

Dear God, help me produce good fruit. Amen.

TUESDAY

Mark 10:23-31

Several years ago, some of my pastor friends posted a picture on social media of a huge mansion obviously worth millions of dollars. It belongs to a famous pastor who broadcasts his church's worship services on television.

Several people made critical comments suggesting perhaps that no pastor should live in such an expensive house. I made a comment on the site about my feelings regarding that situation. Then I wrote: "Then I think about all those people I've met in places like India and Sri Lanka who live in mud huts and wonder what they think of my house."

Mark 10 describes a man who came to Jesus and knelt before him. He asked Jesus an extremely important question: "What must I do to obtain eternal life?" (Mark 10:17). Jesus' answer was pretty much the same as any rabbi of that time would have given: Keep God's commandments.

The man responded to Jesus by insisting that he had kept these commandments since he was a boy. This indicates he honestly believed that he was successfully keeping all of God's laws. This was not unusual, as many religious Jews would have thought the same thing. However, apparently something was making him feel that there was more he should be doing.

Jesus' response addressed the issue that tends to be the spiritual hang-up for many people. We live in a material world that provides many detractions and enormous temptations.

These hinder our spiritual growth. The author of 1 Timothy addressed this issue (1 Timothy 6:6-10). This seems to have been the problem for the man who approached Jesus. People like him need to take the further advice found in 1 Timothy: "Tell people who are rich at this time not to become egotistical and not to place their hope on their finances, which are uncertain. Instead, they need to hope in God, who richly provides everything for our enjoyment. Tell them to do good, to be rich in the good things they do, to be generous, and to share with others" (1 Timothy 6:17-18).

Dear God, help me keep my priorities in proper order. Amen.

WEDNESDAY
Matthew 4:12-22

Eutheos. It is the Greek word we translate as "immediately," or "right away." It is a word we expect to find in the Gospel of Mark, and in fact it does not appear in only three chapters in that whole Gospel (Chapters 12, 13, and 16). In Matthew, however, it is used more sparingly, only 18 times. As a result, it is noticeable when Mark doesn't use this word, but it is also noticeable when Matthew does.

And in this passage, *eutheos* is noticeable, because under what possible circumstances would a person just walk away from his or her whole life to follow a man calling from the lakeshore? I mean, Simon Peter, Andrew, James, and John left their boats, their nets, their livelihoods, and their families and went off to follow Jesus immediately!

I puzzle over this story, but then I remember my own call to ministry. It came in the middle of a career that I loved in a life I was comfortable living. But when the call came, there would be no other way to be happy than to serve Jesus full-time. Now, my acceptance of that call was immediate, but the logistics of making it happen would take another 13 years! That was because I needed to be equipped. That was not immediate, by any means.

Sometimes I feel terrible that it took so long to be equipped. I dragged my feet before I actually entered seminary. I also stayed in school four extra years in order to get a PhD. But you know what? I then served in a cross-academic and pastoral position for the Arkansas Conference of The United Methodist Church. Perhaps all that time is exactly what Jesus called me to.

I also think I have to cut myself some slack. Yes, it took me a while to get equipped, but the disciples had a serious edge: 24-hour-a-day contact with Jesus for three years. I might have gotten more done in those circumstances too. Jesus equipped them in the ways they needed and equipped me in ways I needed as well.

But in the midst of all this equipping, I also realize that Jesus worked with what I already had. He knew I loved school, and he worked with that. Now he is using that. In the same way, Jesus worked with who Simon, Andrew, John, and James were. After all, when he called them, he promised to show them how to fish for people. He was going to take who they already were and what they already knew and put it to work for the Kingdom.

Jesus will do the same for you. Jesus is calling you to something, something you already partially know, and something he will then equip you fully for. All you have to do is be willing to get out of the boat.

Amazing, attentive Jesus, work with what I have to equip me to do your work in the world. Amen.

THURSDAY

1 Corinthians 12:12-13;
Colossians 3:12-17

When I think of bodybuilding, I think of going to the gym and working out for an untold number of hours. I have never had that kind of discipline. In all honesty, I have never had the kind of discipline that keeps me going to the gym once a week, even though I enjoy my time there. For some reason, I do not think it is a priority.

The two passages for our reading today are not about going to the gym, but they are about bodybuilding. The Colossians passage talks about building the kind of person we each should be. We can dress this body up with "compassion, kindness, humility, gentleness, and patience" (Colossians 3:12). We don't always think of those as disciplines that can be cultivated, like muscles that can be shaped by working out, but they are. We may be born with tendencies toward those traits, but they are developed through the choices we make in how we treat one another.

How do we build those traits? Colossians tells us that as well: by allowing the peace of Christ to control our hearts. The Greek word for peace is *eiréné*, and like its Hebrew equivalent *shalom*, it means wholeness, everything in order. This kind of peace speaks of a life oriented around Christ. That takes the same kind of discipline as going to the gym every day. It means making conscious decisions to treat the people around us with kindness and compassion and doing so in a humble and patient way.

While Colossians encourages us to think in terms of individual discipline, 1 Corinthians 12 deals with building the body of Christ. That work is not individual, but communal. Paul reminds us that all the parts of the body are needed, and some parts of the body can't decide that they don't need other parts. In order for the body of Christ to be whole, all the parts must be present. Otherwise, *eiréné* is not possible.

We have come full circle. We should channel the peace of Christ in order to cultivate traits of a disciple of Christ, and then we must work together with our fellow disciples as the body of Christ in order to remain whole and at peace.

The problem, of course, like the discipline of going to the gym, is that such work has to be a priority. It has to be a priority of the individuals, and it has to be a priority of the whole body of Christ. That takes accountability.

There is a reason the gym encourages me to bring a friend, and my gym even lets me do that for free. They know that when someone comes with me, I will stay more committed. We need the same in our discipleship bodybuilding. We need friends, a community of people, who will encourage us along the way as we become the body and bodies Jesus needs us to be.

Dear Jesus, encourage us to stay on the healthy path of discipleship. Amen.

FRIDAY

Matthew 28:16-20

A few years ago, the Barna Group, the leading research organization on the state of church in the United States, released a somewhat shocking statistic: 51 percent of all churchgoers do not know the Great Commission.[1]

I was surprised by this statistic, so I decided to poll some members of my family. One person said, "Go and do something for Jesus, right?" Roughly. A teenager I asked just looked at me like I was speaking another language.

Uh oh. Looks like, as an ordained elder in the church, I had dropped the ball with my own family. I could not imagine that members of my church family would do any better.

These are the parting words Jesus gave to us, our commandment from him, and here some lifelong disciples had a rough or no idea what that was. If we do not know what the Great Commission is, how can we possibly do it? Could the drop in church attendance be as simple as that? Well, no, there are many complicating factors as to why people do not attend church. Even "regular" churchgoers are defined as people who attend church once a month now, according to the book published by the Barna group entitled *Churchless*. If people aren't there to hear the Great Commission talked about, then they won't learn about it. But, also, I think the church has taken for granted that everyone knows it already.

"Baptizing." "Teaching." Of the people who would recognize

the Great Commission, the majority of them would likely stop before the bit about teaching. Without teaching about Jesus, however, we lose the transformative power of the commission.

How many times have we seen a new person get baptized into the church but then quickly fade away from that commitment? Perhaps that is because there was not a clear path for growing in our discipleship. Perhaps the emphasis was on the initial success, one more good number for annual reports on how many were baptized, but no clear way to reorient someone toward a life of discipleship. That is, of course, only if there was an impetus to go and baptize in the first place, but more and more churches now go for years without a single baptism. No wonder we have forgotten what we are called to do. We rarely see it anymore. "Therefore, go and make disciples of all nations, baptizing them in the name of the Father and of the Son and of the Holy Spirit, teaching them to obey everything that I've commanded you" (Matthew 28:19-20). We should all learn it. But more than that, we should all live it.

Lord Jesus, inspire me to go, make disciples, bring them to baptism, and teach them what you command. Amen.

1. "51% of Churchgoers Don't Know of the Great Commission," Barna, *Research Releases in Faith & Christianity*, March 27, 2018, https://www.barna.com/research/half-churchgoers-not-heard-great-commission/.

SATURDAY

Luke 15:11-24

As we reflect on this well-known story about the son who wasted his inheritance on extravagant living, we should remember that a parable is told to make a single point. It is not an allegory that contains hidden meanings through symbolic actions or imagery. The central message of this beautiful parable is this: God loves sinners and welcomes all who repent into his kingdom.

There is nothing in the story that suggests that the son was an evil man. He was simply like a lot of us, especially in our youth. He was tired of always having to do what his parents expected. He wanted to live his own life; do his own thing.

The younger brother had the same problem his older brother had. They both were thinking about themselves, not their father, and certainly not about their brother. This is the root cause of most of our sin.

In his letter to the church at Rome Paul wrote, "So, brothers and sisters, because of God's mercies, I encourage you to present your bodies as a living sacrifice that is holy and pleasing to God. This is your appropriate priestly service. Don't be conformed to the patterns of this world, but be transformed by the renewing of your minds so that you can figure out what God's will is—that is good and pleasing and mature. Because of the grace that God gave me, I can say to each one of you: don't think of yourself more highly than you ought to think" (Romans 12:1-3a).

I once read about a Moorish Palace that had signs out front advertising the wonders and beauties found inside. However, visitors discovered only mirrors. Every direction an individual turned she saw only reflections of herself. Each mirror distorted the image in some way. One mirror would make the person appear tall and thin. Another made the individual appear short and fat. Still another would distort in some other grotesque way. The mirrors would lure the visitor in certain directions, promising an exit, but would only lead to another mirror with another distorted self-image.

In this world it is easy to live in a Moorish Palace where all we see is a distorted image of ourselves. We can easily be fooled into thinking more highly of ourselves than we should.

The younger brother finally came to his senses. He finally saw himself for what he had become. He repented. He turned his life around and went home to his loving father who received him with open arms. It is a beautiful story about God's love for sinners like you and me. The story tells us that the younger brother came to his senses. We don't know if the older brother did or not.

Dear God, help me recognize my selfish nature and give me the wisdom to seek your grace. Amen.

3

A GRACIOUS HEART

The Third Sunday in Lent

Luke 15:11-24

"A certain man had two sons" (Luke 15:11). You know the story already. The prodigal son. This story is sometimes called the gospel-in-miniature. You can probably tell the rest of it yourself.

James Forbes used to tell of a preacher who gave a 16-week sermon series on the prodigal son. Sixteen weeks! At the end of it, he was greeted at the door by a woman who said, "I'm so sorry that poor boy ever ran away from home."[1]

Did you know that the word *prodigal* means "wastefully extravagant"? Clearly, the connotation is that the younger son was wastefully extravagant with his inheritance. "There, he wasted his wealth through extravagant living" (verse 13).

53

But there was someone else who was wastefully extravagant in the story. The father. He threw a lavish party with a fattened calf, a delicacy usually reserved for a great feast day. He was extravagant in welcoming his son. The best robe! A ring! Sandals! But the greatest extravagance came in the father's grace as he restored his relationship with his son.

Some people have a father like the one in the story. Others don't. What Jesus teaches us here is something more than a parenting lesson. It's a lesson about Jesus' own heart for the lost.

Losing

In early 1967, Paul McCartney and John Lennon saw a story in the newspaper about a girl who had run away from home. Inspired by the story, they developed the song "She's Leaving Home" on the album *Sgt. Pepper's Lonely Hearts Club Band*.[2]

In the song, the teenage girl awoke before her parents, left them a note, and snuck down to the kitchen and out of the house. The second verse tells how the parents reacted. There was little concern for their daughter's disappearance.

The chorus, which McCartney and Lennon sang together, continued the parents' lament. But, again, they were most upset that she would do this to them.[3]

It doesn't take long to see that the girl was unhappy in her home. Perhaps there were family dysfunctions or other factors involved. Some listeners to the Beatles' song can identify with it. Anyone can sense the tragedy in it: the unexpected departure of a child.

In Jesus' parable, the younger son left home, but he didn't

sneak out. He boldly asked his father for his inheritance. This was considered disrespectful for a young man to do. The son was treating the father as if he had already died. Most English versions of Luke 15:12 say that the father divided his "estate" between his two sons. But the word for "estate" is actually *bios* ("life") in the New Testament Greek.

"The family therapist in me is wondering about and imagining the breakfast table conversation between Mom and Dad and wondering if Dad is 'enabling' this kid in such a way as almost to guarantee his failure," writes J. William Harkins in *Feasting on the Gospels.*[4]

With his pockets full of money and his father's life broken, the young man traveled to "a land far away" (verse 13). To Jesus' first audience, the implication was clear: The son had gone to Gentile country. There he "wasted his wealth" (verse 13) and, according to the older brother, was "gobbling up [the father's] estate on prostitutes" (verse 30). This, too, was an affront. A proverb of the time said, "A man who loves wisdom makes his father rejoice, but one who spends time with prostitutes destroys riches" (Proverbs 29:3).

Then there was the issue of the son's employment. No self-respecting Jew would work for a Gentile, "one of the citizens of that country" (Luke 15:15). And he certainly wouldn't take a job feeding pigs, for he knew that the pig was unclean (Leviticus 11:7; Deuteronomy 14:8). But here was the younger son, feeding the pigs and even being envious of how much they had to eat (Luke 15:16)!

Life seldom got much lower than this for a first-century Jew.

When have you felt farthest from God? Have you ever run away from God?

Lost

"The milk-cartons program ran its course," said Gaylord Walker to *The Orlando Sentinel* in 2010.[5] Walker was the vice president of the National Child Safety Council, the organization that first put the pictures and descriptions of missing children on milk cartons.

Back when the milk-carton program started in 1984, few good ways existed to get the word out to the public that a child had gone missing. Most people received their news from the half-hour evening television newscast or from their local newspaper. But by the time the news was broadcast or the paper was printed, an abductor could have crossed a few state lines.

Now we have AMBER Alerts in the media and on smartphones. These instant notifications have resulted in 1,114 children being rescued as of May 2, 2022.[6]

But it's safe to assume that the main notification system for missing children in Jesus' time was word of mouth. The way Jesus told the story, the younger son was in "a land far away" (verse 13). As previously mentioned, this would appear to be Gentile country.

So Jesus didn't say anything about the father going to look for the son. Given the limitations of the time, such an effort might have been futile or even dangerous. But we shouldn't assume that the father was indifferent to his son's absence. In fact, when the son eventually returned, the father was exuberant in receiving him (verses 20b-24).

To the father, the younger son was a missing person, and he may have had the same misery parents feel today if their son or daughter has gone missing. But he also had the anguish of knowing that his son was lost. Not all who are lost are missing.

Christians sometimes speak of "the lost." The father in our parable twice refers to his son who was "lost" but is now "found" (verses 24, 32). And you are probably reminded of the lyric in the first verse of "Amazing Grace": "I once was lost, but now am found."[7]

But what do we mean when we say someone is lost? Do we mean the unchurched? Are we referring to those who are not professing Christians? Does it mean those who recklessly sin? All of the above? John Wesley believed that the younger son's chief problem was an "independency on God."[8] He didn't need the father or the father's providence. This was the beginning of his lostness. The dissolute living and the eating with ritually unclean hogs were further expressions of his separation from God.

Commentator R. Alan Culpepper writes, "The younger son's actions report his progressive estrangement from his family, mismanagement of his inheritance, and descent into poverty and privation."[9]

But, like God, the father waited for the lost son to return. We don't know exactly how long the son was away. But the implication is that the father would have waited his whole life. No matter how far we go from God and no matter how long we are away, God will still welcome us home.

Can you identify with the lost son? Can you identify with the father? How?

Found

The younger son's return to his father didn't actually begin when "he got up and went to his father" (Luke 15:20). It began earlier, when "he came to his senses" (verse 17). This was the beginning of his repentance.

It took a famine to push the son to his breaking point. He thought about how well his father's workers ate back home. But when he actually decided to go home, he didn't go home just to get food. He went home to confess his sin, repent, and seek to be accepted, if only as a hired hand.

Joachim Jeremias has commented that "repentance means learning to say Abba again, putting one's whole trust in the heavenly Father, returning to the Father's house and the Father's arms."[10]

The Bible includes several characters who left home only to repent and return later. For example, Jacob prayed for God's help as he tried to go home again: "I don't deserve how loyal and truthful you've been to your servant" (Genesis 32:10). Hear the resemblance to the younger son's speech?

Our parable has become so comfortably familiar that, if we're not careful, we might lose the capacity to be surprised when the son gets closer to home. Remember that the father was not required to forgive and welcome his son.

Jesus' first audience knew what would happen next in the parable: The father would maintain his dignity. The son was dead to him, since the son had treated the father as dead. Maybe, if he was especially merciful, the father would let the son work as a hired hand. At least that's how it was supposed to happen.

But the father saw his son "a long way off." He was "moved with compassion . . . ran to him, hugged him, and kissed him" (Luke 15:20)! The kiss symbolized the father's forgiveness, like when David kissed Absalom (2 Samuel 14:33). Then the father gave his son gifts and threw a party!

It has been noted that all major world religions provide for the wayward to come home again. But not all suggest that there be a party.[11] As Jesus said several verses before today's text, "There will be more joy in heaven over one sinner who changes both heart and life than over ninety-nine righteous people who have no need to change their hearts and lives" (Luke 15:7).

Still shocked over this reception, the son started his well-rehearsed speech: "Father, I have sinned against heaven and against you. I no longer deserve to be called your son" (verse 21). But he didn't get to say the rest (verse 19) before the dad was showering him with gifts: the best robe, a ring, sandals, and a feast.

Each of these gifts was symbolic in its own right. But together they meant that the young man had been restored to his original sonship, a blessing he had not even presumed to ask for. The whole community was to now treat him as the son he once was.

In the same way, God gracefully welcomes the lost. Like the father in this parable, God takes great pleasure when we return. Not only are they found, they are also alive. "We must celebrate with feasting because this son of mine was dead and has come back to life!" (verses 23-24)

This parable comes just after two short parables about

things lost and found: the lost sheep (verses 4-7) and the lost coin (verses 8-10). But neither of those mentions death and life. The parable of the lost son does. Today we are reminded that to be with God is to be alive in the fullest sense.

North Carolina son and acclaimed singer-songwriter James Taylor tells the story of how his father rescued him from a bad part of New York City in the summer of 1967. Taylor had been playing gigs with his band when a record deal fell through and the money dried up. He had a serious drug habit, and he remembers going to sleep to the sound of glass breaking as apartments were burglarized. "I could have disappeared down the drain quite easily at that point," he reveals.

In desperation, Taylor talked to his father on the phone, and his father told him to stay where he was. He immediately drove some 13 hours to New York to get him. They returned to North Carolina, and Taylor sobered up.

"He knew that I was in trouble, and he dropped everything," the artist recalls. "And he himself came. . . . I'll never forget that."[12]

One of the things this text challenges us to do is to develop a heart for the lost like Jesus has. He is the one who has shown us the God who immediately runs to lost sons and daughters, embraces them, and celebrates their return.

Remember who is speaking: Jesus Christ himself. He is not just telling us about God. God is in him.

As the late Peter Gomes once said of this parable, "This is the heart of the gospel and Jesus' message: no one is too far gone, too low, too abased, too bad to be removed from the unconditional love of the Father, not even the baddest of the bad."[13]

Whom do you know who is lost? How can you emulate the waiting father for them?

God of the lost and the found, thank you for patiently waiting for me when I am far from you. Thank you for embracing me when I return to you. Please grant me such grace in my relationship with others. Amen.

1. As told to Peter J. Gomes in *Strength for the Journey* (San Francisco: HarperOne, 2004); page 236.
2. From *Paul McCartney: Many Years From Now*, by Paul McCartney and Barry Miles (Paris: Flammarion, 1997); page 316.
3. From "She's Leaving Home," by Paul McCartney and John Lennon on *Sgt. Pepper's Lonely Hearts Club Band* (London: EMI Studios, 1967).
4. From *Feasting on the Gospels—Luke*, Volume 2, edited by Cynthia A. Jarvis and E. Elizabeth Johnson (Louisville, Kentucky: Westminster John Knox Press, 2014); page 88.
5. From "Remember Missing Kids on Milk Cartons? Short-Lived Idea Built Long-Term Awareness," by Bianca Prieto in *The Orlando Sentinel* (January 10, 2010) at articles.orlandosentinel. com/2010-01-05/news/1001040116_1 _cartons-missing-children-milk.
6. From "AMBER Alert—America's Missing: Broadcast Emergency Response" (2017) at amberalert.gov/.
7. John Newton, "Amazing Grace," *The United Methodist Hymnal*, no. 378, stanza 1.
8. From *John Wesley's Notes on the Whole Bible*, by John Wesley (Christian Classics Ethereal Library, 1765); XV:12.
9. From *The New Interpreter's Bible*, Volume IX; page 301.
10. From *New Testament Theology*, by Joachim Jeremias (Charles Scribner's Sons, 1971); page 156.
11. From *Feasting on the Gospels—Luke*; page 90.
12. From "The Day James Taylor's Father Rescued Him in New York City," on OWN Network (2015) at youtube.com/watch?v=sCMgXi2Z7Zw.
13. From *Strength for the Journey*, by Peter J. Gomes (HarperOne, 2004); page 238.

MONDAY

Ephesians 2:1-10

I read once about a university professor who was invited to speak at a military base in December where he met a soldier named Ralph. This young man had been sent to meet him at the airport. After introducing himself they headed for the baggage claim area. As they made their way there, Ralph kept getting sidetracked. He first stopped to help an older woman whose suitcase had fallen open. On another occasion he lifted two toddlers up to see Santa. Once he stopped to give directions to someone who appeared not to know their way.

Finally the professor asked, "Where did you learn to do that?" "What?" the soldier responded. "Where did you learn to live like that? Taking so much time for people," the professor explained.

"Oh well," Ralph said. "I guess it was during the war in Vietnam." He went on to explain that it had been his job to clear the mine fields and he had watched many of his friends get blown up in front of his eyes. "I learned to live between the steps," he went on. "I never knew when one step might be my last, so I learned to get everything I can out of the moment between when I pick up my foot and when I put it down again."

This soldier's view of the world had been transformed by his experiences in Vietnam. The Christian's view of the world has been transformed by Jesus Christ. Or, at least, it should be. Paul wrote to the church at Ephesus, "You used to live like people of this world. . . . All of you used to do whatever felt good" (verses 2, 3). But God had transformed their lives and given them a new vision of how life should be lived.

Paul went on to insist that Christians are created to do good things. We should live our lives the way Ralph had learned to live his, making every minute count for the cause of Christ.

In verse 8 Paul wrote, "You are saved by God's grace because of your faith." This verse has often been used to argue that we are not saved "by works" but "by faith." On the other hand, the Book of James places the emphasis upon works. "My brothers and sisters, what good is it if people say they have faith but do nothing to show it?" (James 2:14).

However, both James and Paul agree that "faith without actions has no value at all" (James 2:20b). Paul insisted that we are saved by faith, but he also insisted that our new life in Christ should always produce good works. It really is a "What comes first, the chicken or the egg?" kind of question. Both would agree with Jesus who proclaimed, "Not everybody who says to me, 'Lord, Lord,' will get into the kingdom of heaven. Only those who do the will of my Father who is in heaven will enter" (Matthew 7:21).

Dear God, help me learn to live between the steps. Amen.

| **TUESDAY** |

Ezekiel 34:11-16

The priest-prophet Ezekiel was taken into captivity in Babylon during the first deportation of Judah's elite classes in 597 BC. His book is full of mystical visions and prophecies that include references to images that the modern reader finds strange.

Ezekiel 1–24 contains oracles that describe the prophet's call and proclaim dreadful judgment on Judah. Chapters 25–32 contain oracles that condemn foreign nations. This section ends with the fall of Jerusalem. The third division, Chapters 33–39, describes Ezekiel's recommissioning (Chapter 33) and includes oracles and visions of Israel's rebirth. Finally, Chapters 40–48 deal with the future restoration of the Temple.

With Chapter 34, Ezekiel pivots from his visions of judgment and focuses on the future of Israel. The prophet does not foresee the restoration of the Davidic monarchy but does foretell that God will send a descendant of David who will serve as a shepherd to God's people.

This third division ends with Chapter 39, where the author predicts that God will bring his people back from captivity: "So the Lord God proclaims: Now I will bring back the captives of Jacob. I will have compassion on the whole house of Israel and defend my holy name. . . . When I bring them back from the peoples and gather them from the lands of their enemies, I will be made holy through them in the sight of the many nations"

(39:25, 27). Our Scripture for today focuses on a beautiful metaphor where God acts as a shepherd who takes care of God's sheep. We might at once think about Psalm 23.

We might also think about the parable Jesus told as recorded in Matthew 18 and Luke 15. This is a story about a shepherd who left his flock of 99 sheep to find the one that was lost. John's Gospel tells us that Jesus sometimes referred to himself as a shepherd. "I am the good shepherd. The good shepherd lays down his life for the sheep" (John 10:11).

Ezekiel foresaw God leading the Jewish people out of bondage in Babylon like a shepherd leads his sheep. God would do this because it was the just thing to do. God would defend the lost, the wounded, and the weak against the rich and the powerful. God was watching over God's people 2,500 years ago and is still watching over us today.

Dear God, thank you for being my shepherd, for rescuing me and leading me day by day. Amen.

| **WEDNESDAY** |

Hosea 11:1-4, 8-9

The Book of Hosea is the first of the 12 books of the Minor Prophets. (Minor Prophets aren't named minor because of their lack of importance but because of their shorter length.) Hosea prophesied during the last tumultuous years of the Northern Kingdom of Israel, shortly before the fall of Samaria in 722 BC. He was the only prophet native to the Northern Kingdom whose writings have survived. Hosea used an extended metaphor of a troubled marriage to illustrate God's troubled relationship with Israel. He compared the people of Israel to an unfaithful spouse. The prophet urged the people to turn from their sin and to return to God's compassionate embrace.

The first three chapters of the book describe Hosea's marriage and compare it to God's relationship with the Israelites. Both were loving husbands who had been betrayed by their wives. God had delivered his bride Israel from bondage in Egypt only to be spurned by their worship of Baal, the Canaanite fertility god.

Hosea even began his book by claiming that God had instructed him to enter into an unholy marriage to illustrate to the people how they had treated God. "'Go, marry a prostitute and have children of prostitution, for the people of the land commit great prostitution by deserting the LORD.' So Hosea went and took Gomer, Diblaim's daughter, and she became pregnant and bore him a son" (Hosea 1:2-3).

The Book of Hosea uses poetic language of passion and emotional sentiment to reveal God's love for the people. It depicts God as being angry and hurt because they had rejected God and gone after other gods.

In today's text, Hosea described the people's sin and how God wanted to restore their relationship because of God's love for them. Like many parents, I can understand something of what is going on here at a deep level. I have an adult child I am proud of. However, there was a time when this child brought me great heartache. As a teenager, she made poor choices. Of course, I never stopped loving her; and I would like to think that God's love, my love, and her mother's love is at least part of what helped bring about her spiritual, emotional, and physical restoration.

There is no greater power than the power of love. Do you know someone who needs a change of heart? Perhaps it's a family member, a coworker, or even your boss. The greatest tool you have to help change their life is your love—your compassion. The more unlovable they are, the more they need your undeserved, unconditional love. The less love they show for you, the more they need your understanding and caring. God loved the people of Israel, God loves you, and God calls you to love others.

Dear God, teach me to love others as you have loved all people. Amen.

THURSDAY

Luke 3:12-13; 5:27-32

Great fishermen know where to catch fish. They understand the needs of fish. They take into account that fish need protection from predators so they are more often found around trees, bushes, and submerged rocks. An experienced fisherman knows how to read the currents. And, of course, fish are more likely to be found where food is present.

Earlier in Luke 5, we read that Jesus got into Simon's boat, sat down, and spoke to the people. Afterward, he asked Simon (later called Peter) to row further out into the lake and let down his nets. Simon thought this would be a waste of time, but he agreed to do so. They caught so many fish that their nets were tearing, and they had to call for help to gather all the fish. The boat was so full it almost sank.

Luke tells us that Peter was so amazed he fell at Jesus' feet and cried out, "Leave me, Lord, for I'm a sinner!" Jesus responded, "Don't be afraid. From now on, you will be fishing for people." Then, Luke says, "As soon as they brought the boats to the shore, they left everything and followed Jesus" (Luke 5:8, 10, 11).

Jesus called his disciples to fish for people, and Jesus knew how to catch these "human fish." He didn't go about looking for his catch among the most religious or most honorable. Most religious teachers probably looked for students in the synagogues and among the more respected members of society. Jesus sought out the outcast, the last, the lost, the least, and the hated. Levi was one of the hated. Jesus insisted that he came to call sinners to change their hearts and lives. He recognized that we do not reach people when we separate ourselves from them. We reach them when we build relationships with them. An old adage says, "People don't care how much you know until they know how much you care." Jesus understood this. People sometimes read the stories about how Jesus called his disciples and assume that these accounts tell us the whole story. It's entirely possible that these occasions were not the first times Peter and Levi had encountered Jesus. Jesus may well have established a trusting relationship before he finally "pulled in his catch." Regardless, Levi left behind his well-paying job and his affluent lifestyle in response to Jesus' call to "Follow me."

Sometimes the church makes the same mistake that the Pharisees and the legal experts in Jesus' day made. We gather into our little enclaves, separating ourselves from the very ones God has called us to reach. And then we wonder why our evangelistic methods aren't working.

Dear God, give me the compassion exemplified by Jesus for the last, the lost, and the least. Amen.

FRIDAY

Luke 15:1-10

It is possible that Jesus may have tried reaching people in the synagogues early in his ministry; the Bible does not tell us. He may have tried first to convince Pharisees and Sadducees and legal experts they needed to radically change their thinking. If he did, he no doubt quickly found them unresponsive.

In yesterday's text, we read where Jesus said, "Healthy people don't need a doctor, but sick people do" (Luke 5:31). People who think they are spiritually healthy don't think they need to change. The Pharisees thought they were spiritually healthy and didn't need to make the changes Jesus was calling for.

One of the problems with being religious is that one may confuse claiming certain beliefs and practicing certain religious rituals with actually being righteous. I once heard the Quaker theologian Elton Trueblood say something like, "Many Christians have just enough religion to inoculate them against the real thing."

People who know they are sinners and fall far short of who they should be are often more willing to genuinely confess their sin and make real changes in their lives. Jesus must have discovered that there were better prospects among the outcasts than among those who felt like they had life under control. The poor and disenfranchised are usually hurting more and may feel a greater need for change.

The parables in today's Scripture remind us how important

each one of us is to God. Three chapters earlier, Luke records Jesus saying, "Aren't five sparrows sold for two small coins? Yet not one of them is overlooked by God. Even the hairs on your head are all counted. Don't be afraid. You are worth more than many sparrows" (12:6-7).

God loves you. You are of infinite worth to God. So is your neighbor and your colleague at work. So is the lady at the checkout counter at the grocery store and the homeless man you occasionally see on the street. God loves every individual and wants everyone to enjoy a full and meaningful life. He loves those who practice religions other than ours and those who practice no religion.

God made each of us with a unique fingerprint. We are all uniquely gifted, and we are all created in God's image. The first chapter of the Bible tells us, "God created humanity in God's own image, in the divine image God created them, male and female God created them" (Genesis 1:27).

Many of us memorized John 3:16 when we were children. It tells us that God loved each of us so much that he gave Jesus willingly to die on our behalf. First Timothy 2:4 reminds us that God "wants all people to be saved and to come to a knowledge of the truth."

Dear God, fill me with your compassion for those who are lost. Amen.

SATURDAY

Luke 19:1-10

At the beginning of this week (page 60), you read the story about the famous singer-songwriter James Taylor. He was living in New York City in the summer of 1967. Things were going quite well for him until a record deal fell through and he had no more money.

With nowhere else to turn, he called his father. To his amazement, his dad immediately drove 13 hours, picked him up, and took him home to North Carolina. Taylor never forgot that his father immediately dropped everything to come and get him.

Today's Scripture text tells us that Jesus "came to seek and save the lost." Zacchaeus was successful as the world measures success. However, he must have realized that something was missing in his life. Why else would he go to such lengths to see Jesus?

The text we have doesn't tell us all the details of this story. What we do see is a man who made a radical change in his behavior because of his encounter with Jesus. What we do see is a new creature in Christ who decided to live by a radically different set of values.

Just a few verses earlier in Luke's Gospel, we read that Jesus said, "It's very hard for the wealthy to enter God's kingdom! It's easier for a camel to squeeze through the eye of a needle than for a rich person to enter God's kingdom" (Luke 18:24b-25).

Today we read about the camel who made it through that eye!

We should be careful about giving up on people. "That's ole Joe. He is the town drunk. He'll never change." "Sue's husband never comes to church. And he never will."

When I was appointed as pastor to a new church, I always spent a great deal of my time the first six months visiting inactive church members. Sometimes other church members had given up on them. I also tried to keep my eyes open for those people who never went to church but seemed to have things going on in their lives that brought discontent.

James Taylor's life was apparently changed by the compassionate act of a loving father. Zacchaeus was changed by the attention Jesus gave him.

When Jesus told the disciples how difficult it is for a wealthy person to enter God's kingdom, they asked, "Then who can be saved?" Jesus replied, "What is impossible for humans is possible for God" (Luke 18:26-27). We need to look for those around us like Zacchaeus who are open to change and join God in transforming work.

Dear God, use me today to touch the life of a lost Zacchaeus. Amen.

4

A HEART FOR SEEKERS

The Fourth Sunday in Lent

Luke 19:1-10

What do you know about Zacchaeus? That he was short, of course. Anyone who grew up going to Sunday school or vacation Bible school knows the old song: "Zacchaeus was a wee little man, and a wee little man was he."[1]

But what if I were to tell you that we can't know for sure that Zacchaeus was short? "It's right there in the text," you say. Luke does state that Zacchaeus "was trying to see who Jesus was, but, being a short man, he couldn't because of the crowd" (Luke 19:3).

Yet the way ancient Greek grammar works, we can't be absolutely positive that the Greek word for "short" should be applied to Zacchaeus. Technically, it could just as easily be applied to Jesus! Then it would mean that Jesus was hard to see because Jesus was short, thus leading Zacchaeus to climb a tree to see Jesus over people's heads.[2]

You very well may not like the idea of a short Jesus. I'm not sure I do. When I hear that he "grew in wisdom and stature" (Luke 2:52, NIV), I like to imagine him growing tall. But then I remember that the Greek word for "stature" can also mean longevity. So some translations say he "matured in wisdom and years" (Luke 2:52, CEB).

Yes, it's all Greek to me, too!

So what difference does Jesus' height make? It doesn't make any difference for Jesus. His power doesn't come from his height. But I believe it makes a difference if we have trouble accepting a short Jesus. I believe we have an innate bias that associates height with authority. So a short Jesus can sound strange to us, maybe off-putting. But today's text teaches that Jesus came to bring salvation to all, regardless of height or, in this case, occupation. So we shouldn't be like the crowd that exhibited a bias saying, "He has gone to be the guest of a sinner" (19:7). Jesus demonstrated to the crowd that the salvation he brought was for all—even tax collectors, short or tall.

We Are the Crowd

What else do you know about Zacchaeus? That he was a tax collector. But did you know that tax collectors weren't like the IRS agents of today? In Jesus' time, Roman officials contracted with local people to collect taxes, tolls, and tariffs. But the

Romans didn't pay those contractors a salary. So tax collectors extorted their own wages from those they shook down.

Zacchaeus was not just any tax collector. He must have been good at his job. Luke says that he was a "ruler among tax collectors," and he was "rich" (Luke 19:2).

It's interesting that Luke would take the opportunity here to call Zacchaeus rich. In the preceding chapter, Luke told us about a certain ruler who "became sad because he was extremely rich" when Jesus told him to sell all his possessions and give the money to the poor (18:23). Jesus then said that it would be "easier for a camel to squeeze through the eye of a needle than for a rich person to enter God's kingdom" (18:25)! Luke seemed to want to make sure his readers understand that Jesus had some serious concerns about wealth.

But Jesus then said, "What is impossible for humans is possible for God" (18:27). So if Zacchaeus was going to enter God's kingdom, it was going to take an act of God.

Zacchaeus would have to be like the tax collector in Jesus' brief story about the Pharisee and the tax collector. In that story, coming just a chapter before today's text, a Pharisee and a tax collector "went up to the temple to pray" (18:10). The Pharisee thanked God that he was not like other people. But the tax collector "struck his chest and said, 'God, show mercy to me, a sinner.' I tell you," Jesus said, "this person went down to his home justified rather than the Pharisee" (18:13-14). This was a lesson to "certain people who had convinced themselves that they were righteous and who looked on everyone else with disgust," Luke told his readers (18:9). Interesting! Had these certain people also been in the crowd that surrounded Jesus when he spotted Zacchaeus up in the sycamore tree? Maybe. For we are told that when Jesus announced his plan to visit Zacchaeus's house, "everyone who saw this grumbled" (19:7).

Usually, it was the Pharisees who grumbled about Jesus eating with sinners (15:1-2). But this time it was everyone. The Pharisees aren't mentioned in this case.

And where were the disciples? Luke does not record that they spoke up, either. Could it be that the disciples were even part of the grumbling crowd? They had just come from acting as crowd-control when people tried to bring babies to Jesus (18:15). They had just scolded the blind man who called out to Jesus for mercy (18:38-39).

In both cases, Jesus overrode his disciples. He blessed the children and healed the blind man. So it's possible that the disciples were feeling confused about their role or even frustrated at Jesus by the time they arrived in Jericho. Perhaps the disciples also needed to learn that God offers the gift of salvation to all, even children, blind men, and tax collectors.

As Jesus' modern-day disciples, this lesson is still relevant to us, for we, too, tend to put people in categories. We figure that some people will never change. We might even get upset when Jesus turns his attention to someone we don't like instead of staying to enjoy the party we are throwing for him. Of all the people Jesus could visit in Jericho, he went to the home of a rich man who collaborated with Rome. That was not a crowd-pleaser.

Bishop William Willimon once preached that "the crowd,

the good-enough church-going, Bible-believing, close-friends-with-God folk of Jericho, hated Jesus for" extending salvation to one such as Zacchaeus. The bishop went on to tell of a young man he knew in high school. We'll call him Biff. Will, as the good bishop was known at the time, didn't care much for Biff. Biff seemed to have the attention of the prettiest girls. He was the first to get his own car.

After Biff and Will graduated and went off to different colleges, they lost touch with one another. The bishop confessed that he didn't mind that at all. But then came the high school reunion!

Will was nibbling on a cookie and catching up with old friends when, all of a sudden, Biff came running at him, hugged him, and said, "They tell me you are a preacher! That's great! Would you believe it? I've been born again! I've accepted Jesus into my life and now I'm changed. I go to church every Sunday and I pray every day!"

Will told Biff that he was happy for him, but inside Will was shaken. "Of all the people to have 'accepted Jesus' into his life," he grumbled to himself. Biff!? Of all the people Jesus would visit. Biff!?[3]

So it falls to you and to me to take a long look inward. At one point or another, we are in the crowd that grumbled. What is Jesus teaching us in the crowd? in the church?

Is there someone you just can't imagine Jesus visiting? Could you visit that person in Jesus' name?

We Are Zacchaeus

Zacchaeus was as surprised as anyone! He thought he was going to seek Jesus by going up in that sycamore tree. But Jesus ended up seeking him! "Zacchaeus, come down at once. I must stay in your home today" (Luke 19:5).

My mother always taught me that it was rude to invite yourself over to someone else's house. That was hard to understand when I was young. My friends had different toys than I had. Why couldn't I just ask them if I could come over and play?

"You should wait to be invited," she would remind me. Of course, she was right.

But when I became a pastor, I was afforded a certain amount of license to invite myself to someone else's house when a pastoral visit was in order. But I still try to be courteous about it: "I'd be glad to come over to your house if you'd like, or meet you someplace where we can talk, or you are always welcome to come to my office," I usually say.

Jesus did not need to worry about any of that. He knew his role. He was bringing salvation to Zacchaeus's household (verse 9). It's easy to understand that Zacchaeus was "happy to welcome Jesus" (verse 6). That much is obvious. But consider that Jesus' presence also brought a ritual purity and social dignity to Zacchaeus's house. Every observant Jew knew that a tax collector was always going in and out of Gentile houses and handling unclean things. A rabbi would surely have been sacrificing some of his own ritual purity and social dignity in going to a tax collector's house. Yet visit him, Jesus did.

Not only that, but Jesus' visit offered Zacchaeus restoration in the eyes of the community! And he would later even call Zacchaeus a "son of Abraham" (verse 9). I'm fascinated by what Zacchaeus said to Jesus. In his only line of dialogue, Zacchaeus rushed to defend his dignity and purity of heart: "Look, Lord, I give half of my possessions to the poor. And if I have cheated anyone, I repay them four times as much" (verse 8).

A few weeks ago, I was out walking our family dog in the evening. I walked by the house of neighbor I had not yet met. He was in his driveway. We greeted and introduced ourselves. Our introductions included sharing our occupations, as introductions sometimes do.

When he learned that I am a pastor, he quickly pointed to his cocktail and declared, "I only have one of these every once in a while. You know, I think it's really good to help people. I try to give to the charities around here whenever I can. And if I see a hurt animal, I try to take it to a vet." On and on he went, completely unsolicited.

What was Zacchaeus feeling when he injected his own defense? He answered a question that Jesus hadn't asked. Perhaps he was concerned that the crowd's grumbling was giving Jesus a bad impression. But Jesus' mind was on salvation, not impression or reputation. "Today, salvation has come to this household," Jesus declared (verse 9). What wonderful news! Jesus was bringing salvation to all! And not some other day but today! First it was, "I must stay in your home *today*" (verse 5; italics added); and now, "*Today*, salvation has come to this household" (verse 9; italics added).

The salvation Jesus brings in Luke is immediate. From the angelic pronouncement of his birth (2:11) to Jesus' sermon in Nazareth (4:21) to even the pardon of the criminal on the cross next to him (23:42-43), the salvation of Jesus came "today," and it came for all. The saving love of the Lord will not be limited by time, place, or person!

Can you relate to Zacchaeus? Have you accepted that Jesus' salvation comes to you and comes today?

We Are the Church

Though Luke records that Jesus was having a conversation with Zacchaeus, I suspect that Jesus was probably speaking loudly enough for everyone to hear. In fact, the very next verse says that "they [plural] listened to this" (Luke 19:11). In that way, Zacchaeus could serve as an example to the crowd that he "came to seek and save the lost" (verse 10).

Jesus' message of salvation was never going to remain a matter of private conversation or for one household. He would later tell his disciples that they were to be his "witnesses in Jerusalem, in all Judea and Samaria, and to the end of the earth" (Acts 1:8).

You may recall that the Gospel of Luke and the Acts of the Apostles were written by Luke and were two volumes of one large story. So we should remember that the stories we read in Luke's Gospel lead up to the expansion of God's kingdom through the apostles and the church. We who are the church today take up the mantle of the apostles who believed that

God offers the gift of salvation to all in Jesus Christ, even tax collectors like Zacchaeus.

So how are we doing with that, church? Have we learned what the crowd learned that day in Jericho? Is there any person or any place we just can't imagine Jesus visiting? The crowd thought of Zacchaeus as a crook. Could we imagine Jesus going to visit one of the most notorious criminals today?

Can today's church follow Jesus' example and go into unexpected places to bring his salvation to all? St. Paul United Methodist Church in Abilene, Texas, can serve as an example. They thought about the children in their community and decided to go outside their church walls to bring salvation to all. They partnered with Johnston Elementary School to provide an after-school program. Church leaders noted that their vacation Bible school, while enjoyable and successful, reached a fraction of the children in the community for only one week a year. So they redirected their VBS resources to start an after-school program for 23 weeks of the year. (Perhaps they sing the old Zacchaeus song there too!)

"It's always a surprise what God can do," noted church member Adam Samuels to United Methodist Communications, "when we allow ourselves to be changed and to redirect ourselves back to where we can best reach our community."[4]

Has the church learned what Zacchaeus himself learned? Do we seek Jesus like he did? Do we still see ourselves as seekers? Zacchaeus climbed a tree, something a dignified Palestinian man in the first century usually didn't do. What are we willing to do to seek Jesus?

We just might find that Jesus has been seeking us all along. We might discover that salvation has come to our house today too. And we might even come to realize that salvation comes not because we earned it but because Jesus "came to seek and save the lost," no matter how short or tall we are (Luke 19:10).

In what ways can you, the church, take the love of Jesus to unlikely places in your community?

Seek me out, Lord Jesus. Come into my home and my heart today, and bring your salvation. Then lead me out to unlikely places where I might delight in finding you already there. Amen.

1. Traditional. Author unknown.
2. From "The Short One: Luke 19:1-10," by Roberta Bondi in *The Christian Century*, Volume 121, Number 21 (2004).
3. From "The Wrong People Saved," by William Willimon in *Pulpit Resource*, Volume 44, Number 4 (2016).
4. From "Church's Vacation Bible School Reaches New Kids a New Way," United Methodist Communications at http://ee.umc.org/how-we-serve/churchs-vacation-bible-school-reaches-new-kids-a-new-way (August 2017).

MONDAY

Exodus 22:1-3; Numbers 5:5-7

I once read a story purported to be true. If it isn't true in fact, it is still a great parable worth remembering.

A man owned a flock of chickens he had always kept in a pen. One day, he decided to let them run in his yard. He did so after clipping their wings. A few days later, he came home to learn that an irate neighbor had been there to inform him that the hens had gotten into his garden. The neighbor had killed several of them and had thrown the dead chickens into the man's yard.

The owner of the chickens was furious. He couldn't believe what the neighbor had done. He was determined to get some kind of compensation for his highly valued hens. The man ate his dinner, trying his best to keep his cool. By the time dinner was concluded, he had calmed down enough to think through what had happened. He decided his prized hens weren't worth turning a neighbor into a bitter enemy.

He went over to the neighbor's house and found the enraged man in his garden chasing one of the chickens with his hoe. The owner of the hens approached the gardener, whose face was red with rage. When the gardener saw the man, he shouted, "You have abused me. I will kill all of your hens if I can get them. My garden has been destroyed."

"I'm sorry," the man replied. "I did not wish to injure you, and now I see that I have made a great mistake in letting out my hens. I ask your forgiveness, and I am willing to pay you six times the damage."

The gardener was mystified. He couldn't believe what he had just heard. He stood there propped against his hoe in stunned silence. "Tell me the damage, and I'll repay you sixfold. And I'll make sure my hens never bother you again. I just can't afford to lose the goodwill of my neighbor over a bunch of chickens."

As the gardener gazed up at the sky, he responded, "I am the fool. The damage is hardly worth mentioning. I have more reason to ask your forgiveness than you have to ask of mine."

To those who have ears to hear, let them hear.

The laws of Moses called for restitution when one Israelite wronged another. It is important for any society to make laws that do as much as possible to assure justice. But God calls us to go beyond the Law. We are called to a greater challenge. We are instructed to love our neighbor. Our relationships with God and one another trump any other rule or regulation.

Dear God, fill me with your loving kindness so that in difficult times I might not despair but will submit myself to your holy will. Amen.

TUESDAY

Deuteronomy 26:16-19

The Greeks called the fifth book of the Old Testament *Deuteronomion*, meaning the second law. This is where we get *Deuteronomy*. At the heart of the book is the idea that obedience to the Mosaic laws ensures prosperity and divine protection while disobedience ensures national devastation. The book consists of three discourses or speeches delivered by Moses shortly before his death.

The first speech, in Deuteronomy 1:1–4:40, reviews the major events of the past 40 years in the wilderness. It exhorts the Israelites to obey God's laws and warns against neglecting the God of their fathers.

The second speech (5:1–26:19) contains a lengthy recapitulation of the laws given by God at Mount Sinai. This is where the book gets its name "Second Law." Our Scripture for today is the summary conclusion to this second speech. The regulations and case laws mentioned in Deuteronomy 26:16 are referring to all the laws discussed throughout Chapters 12–26.

While Jesus confirmed that the greatest law is to love God and neighbor, this does not mean that God's people are to ignore the rest of these moral laws (Matthew 5:17-20). It is primarily from the writings of Paul that Protestant Christians get the idea that we are saved by faith, not by works. But this doesn't mean that Paul rejected the laws of God. He wrote to the church at Rome, "Do we then cancel the Law through this faith? Absolutely not! Instead, we confirm the Law" (Romans 3:31).

Many Old Testament laws, including most of those referred to in today's text, served as civil and ceremonial laws for the Israelite people. The laws of God we should be keeping are the moral laws that help us lead a righteous life.

Dear God, write on my heart the laws you want me to keep. Amen.

WEDNESDAY

Luke 4:38-43

People on skid row are not that different from those living in the better neighborhoods of any city. Their sins may generally be more visible, as they are often living in bondage to alcohol and drugs and/or psychological problems. Those living in the more desirable parts of town are often living in bondage to other things that might be less visible. Their addictions haven't yet destroyed their reputation.

To God we are all the same. The universal problem is sin, and God's solution is the same for all men and women. God offers forgiveness to everyone. God's transformational Spirit is available to every individual.

The first step to life transformation by the Spirit of God is admitting that we are sinners in need of God's saving grace. This means we recognize that we are broken and need repair. Of course, this brokenness comes in all kinds of forms: emotional, physical, mental and spiritual.

The Gospel of Luke tells us that Jesus went about healing and teaching. Earlier in Chapter 4, we learn that Jesus went to his home synagogue in Nazareth and read from the prophet Isaiah, announcing that he was the fulfillment of the prophet's proclamation. He had come *"to preach good news to the poor, to proclaim release to the prisoners and recovery of sight to the blind, to liberate the oppressed, and to proclaim the year of the Lord's favor"* (Luke 4:18-19).

After Jesus left Nazareth, he went to Capernaum where he taught the people each sabbath. This was Peter's hometown. Luke tells us that one day Jesus exorcized a demon from a man in the synagogue. Because of this, "reports about [Jesus] spread everywhere in the surrounding region" (verse 37).

After this happened at the synagogue, Jesus went home with Simon Peter. There they found Peter's mother-in-law sick with a fever. After Jesus healed her, his reputation continued to grow. As word got around, more and more people came to Jesus seeking to be healed.

Jesus responded to their physical problems, but he was also interested in healing their spiritual problems. "I must preach the good news of God's kingdom," he told them when they "tried to keep him from leaving them" (verses 42-43).

Some Christians turn Jesus' message into a "social gospel" that speaks only to social injustices. Others insist the good news has to do only with individuals' spiritual conversion. It's about "pie in the sky, by and by." However, the Scripture is quite clear. God is interested in the whole person. God cares about the unemployed and the disenfranchised. God cares about your cancer and about your eternal soul. God cares about the least, the last, and the lost.

Dear God, thank you for your love that knows no boundaries. Amen.

THURSDAY

Luke 18:15-17

As I sit at the computer today, I am keenly aware that it is a special occasion—my granddaughter's birthday. It is not hard to imagine why people were taking their children to Jesus to be blessed by him. If the human Jesus was in town today, I would surely take Kimberly and her little brother, Eli, to be blessed. And if I had lived over 2,000 years ago in an age without modern medicine, it would have been an even greater opportunity.

We are not told in the text why the disciples scolded the parents for bringing their children to Jesus. However, it is not hard to imagine that it was a combination of pride and tradition. Children were not taken seriously. The disciples didn't want to bother Jesus with less important things. They assumed he wanted to use his time for grown-up problems.

Of course, the Gospel writers include these verses because they tell us something about the kingdom of God. Jesus insisted that "God's kingdom belongs to people like these children" (Luke 18:16). We have to become like a child to enter God's kingdom.

What childlike characteristics did Jesus have in mind?

When she was younger, several people asked my granddaughter, "How old are you now?" Each time she immediately responded with a radiant smile and an energetic, "I'm four years old!" Children have an openness and forthrightness that we tend to lose as we grow older. As we age, we tend to become more defensive and prideful.

Kimberly trusts those adults in her life who have always given her loving care. Why wouldn't she? We have always been there for her. We have provided for her every need. We don't give her everything she asks for, but she understands we want what is best for her. She is already learning to ask if a particular food is healthy or not. Even though she sometimes says, "I can do it myself," she knows that she is dependent upon the adults in her life who love her.

As we grow older, we tend to forget these realities. We sometimes forget that we are dependent upon others. It is especially easy to forget that we are dependent upon God. Jesus is telling us that we will never enter the Kingdom until we recognize our dependence upon God. God has given us loving care all of our lives and provides for our needs. We don't receive everything we want because God knows our needs better than we do.

We have already seen in the Gospel of Luke that the kingdom of God belongs to the poor, to the diseased, to the tax collectors, and to the women. Now Luke tells us it belongs to the children who know how to trust.

Dear God, thank you for being like a loving parent and for always being there for me. Amen.

FRIDAY

Luke 18:18-30

I read once about a group of Christians who were meeting secretly in a house church in the Soviet Union. As they quietly sang a hymn, two Soviet soldiers suddenly burst into the room with weapons ready to shoot. One of the soldiers shouted, "If you wish to renounce your Christian faith, you may leave now!" Some of those present left the room quickly. The man shouted, "This is your last chance. Abandon your practice of Christianity and never come back, or stay and suffer the consequences." A few more people exited the room.

After those left, one of the soldiers closed the door and announced, "Keep your hands up—but keep them up in praise to our Lord Jesus."

The two soldiers then explained. Sometime earlier, they had been sent to another house church to arrest the members. However, rather than arresting those worshipping there, the members of the church had led them to faith in Christ. "What we have learned since our conversion is this: Unless a person is willing to die for his or her faith, that individual cannot be completely trusted," the soldiers said.

People who live in a society like the former Soviet Union or communist China probably have a greater comprehension of today's text than do we. Surely, Jesus didn't mean for us to take it as a universal rule that everyone should sell all their possessions and give the proceeds to the poor. If that is the requirement, most of us are in serious trouble with the Lord.

On the other hand, we should not be so quick to assume this requirement was meant only for this particular man and has nothing to do with us. Mark, Matthew, and Luke all include this story in their Gospels. There must be a reason they all thought it important enough to include.

It certainly says something about the radical nature of discipleship. Jesus was looking for a few good men and women who would make a total commitment. Jesus is still looking for those who mean it when they sing, "All to Jesus I surrender; all to him I freely give; I will ever love and trust him, in his presence daily live."[1]

Christian discipleship means avoiding evil. It also means doing good. Most of all it means loving God and submitting our will to God. It means submitting ourselves to the lordship of Jesus Christ and doing whatever he asks us to do, including loving our neighbor as we love ourselves.

Luke tells us that the ruler who talked with Jesus was sad when he went away. Jesus was sad as well, because the wealth the man chose was nothing compared to what God had to offer him.

Dear God, give me the spiritual insight to clearly comprehend the benefits of obedient discipleship. Amen.

1. J. W. Van Deventer, "I Surrender All," *The United Methodist Hymnal*, no. 354, stanza 1.

SATURDAY

Matthew 10:1-15

Why would Jesus choose only 12 people to do his work? It seems like, as long as he was here and as long as these people were going to be responsible for founding the church, maybe he would choose a few more. In fact, in Luke, while Jesus did choose only 12 apostles, he chose 72 to carry out this same mission he gave the 12 in Matthew.

Matthew was more likely to emphasize the 12 because of Matthew's Jewish commitments. We know from the Gospel of Matthew's focus on Jewish law and ritual that Matthew was most likely written for a largely Jewish community. Twelve is significant for Jews because of the 12 tribes of Israel. These 12 apostles would become the new 12 heads of the faith.

And what were these 12 called to do? Some pretty miraculous things, including raising people from the dead. They were also, however, given some pretty strict regulations. Let's deal with a couple of those.

They were not to take any money for their work. Why not? Well, Jesus explained, you did not pay to get this gift of healing; you should not profit from it. It is fine, even appropriate, for such workers to receive a place to stay and food for their work, but nothing additional.

In the first century, there were two kinds of healers: doctors and priests. Neither one was supposed to take money for their work. Taking money almost always meant the person was a crook or a charlatan. The apostles would be doing the work of doctors and priests. They were representing God and God's power. They should not do so under exploitative terms. Also, like the instructions not to take extra clothes, it signaled an intent to rely upon the provision of God and God's people.

The other interesting instruction was to leave peace at a house that offered peace, but to shake dust from the feet of a house that did not return the same sentiment. A greeting of peace (*shalom* in Hebrew) was a wish not just for good health, but for full restoration of someone's soul. Anyone who would not wish such goodness on the apostles was not interested in mutual concern and well-being.

As for the dust, shaking dust off your feet or clothes at someone was a sign of repudiation. Perhaps it grew from the portrayal of dust as a sign of judgment or humiliation from the Hebrew Bible. Perhaps it was just one of those cultural expressions. Either way, it was definitely an insult.

For us, this passage reminds us as disciples ourselves that we are not to exploit God's power, that as God's representatives we are to bring healing to hurting masses, that not everyone will be accepting of what we say or offer, and it only takes a small number of us to change the world.

Send me out in your name, wonderful Jesus, and equip me to do your work in the world. Amen.

5

A PURPOSEFUL HEART

The Fifth Sunday in Lent

Matthew 10:1-15

All of our worldly possessions were traveling down the interstate in the back of a truck driven by a man I'd only just met. It was moving day for pastors in our conference of The United Methodist Church, and our family was moving to my next ministry appointment.

Actually, there were two trucks. The first truck the movers brought wasn't big enough. Perhaps they assumed a pastor would pack light. Maybe we should have. After all, Jesus did say, "Don't take a backpack for the road or two shirts or sandals or a walking stick" (Matthew 10:10).

I follow in the line of circuit rider preachers who had very little to their names. They didn't stay in one place long enough to acquire many possessions. They were always on the move. No pension. No office hours. But here we were with all these things in trucks.

Perhaps we preachers have become too settled, I thought to myself as I drove along behind the moving trucks in one of our two cars, both of them packed with more stuff.

But there in the other car was also the rest of my family. Each of us had stuff. When Jesus told his 12 apostles not to carry money or a change of clothes, did that apply to their families as well? Would Jesus' instructions be different if he were giving them in our time and place? Has the mission changed?

The mission in our time and place usually seems to revolve around getting people to come to the worship service. We often place great emphasis on attracting more people to come and do what we do at church. Should we set up a fancy coffee bar? Would people prefer a projection screen over a hymnal? What would attract them?

There may be Bible verses about inviting people to worship services, but they don't quickly come to my mind. What Jesus did talk about in this text from Matthew 10 was giving his apostles authority and sending them out. To invite people to church? No. To go to other places to proclaim that the kingdom of God has come near and to "heal the sick, raise the dead, cleanse those with skin diseases, and throw out demons" (verse 8). I don't know many Christians who are doing just one of those things, let alone all four!

Yet we can't dismiss the importance of this text. Here we have a rarity: Jesus' specific and direct instructions to his disciples.

No enigmatic teachings or parables. Just straightforward instructions. What to do and what not to do.

We'd better take a close look at what Jesus said!

If They Can Do It . . .

Television streaming services are dangerous. I don't binge-watch, but over the course of several months, I can watch all the episodes of a television show. So far, I've seen all of *Cheers*, *The Dick Van Dyke Show*, *Star Trek* and its spin-offs, and more.

Another old series I've watched is *Mission: Impossible*. In each episode, after Steven Hill or Peter Graves received his secret assignment, he would go through pictures of possible agents and choose his team. Sure, most of them were the same people from week to week, but he chose them based on their various skill sets.

So I sometimes wonder what Jesus saw in the 12 men he picked to be his apostles. Maybe they weren't completely incompetent. But if any of them had any discernable skills applicable to the task at hand, I can't figure out what they were.

Anyone with oratory skills to go up against the best Roman senators? Nope. Influential friends of Herod? I don't see any. Men with deep pockets to support the ministry? No sign of those. In fact, they even had a thief and a betrayer in charge of the money (John 12:6)!

A friend once wrote, "Either Jesus is a miserable judge of character, or even his worst enemies are able to go out and work miracles in his name."[1] My friend and I prefer the latter possibility. Jesus knows that his disciples, whoever they may be, can do "even greater works than these" under his authority (John 14:12).

They would have to. For just before today's text begins, Jesus had compassion on the crowds "because they were troubled and helpless, like sheep without a shepherd" (Matthew 9:36). He told his followers, "The size of the harvest is bigger than you can imagine, but there are few workers" (9:37).

Then Matthew tells us what Jesus did about it. "He called his twelve disciples and gave them authority over unclean spirits to throw them out and to heal every disease and every sickness" (10:1). Did you catch that? He gave them authority to do the very kinds of things he was doing! Compare the list in Matthew 10:1 to the description of Jesus' own ministry in Matthew 9:35. It's basically the same. They were to continue the work he had started (John 14:12), for as the Father sent the Son, so the Son sends his followers (John 20:21).

In the rock opera *Jesus Christ Superstar*, the disciples are in a pensive mood at the Last Supper. They are disappointed that Jesus will let himself be crucified because they believe it will mean the end of their story with him. They wish that they could have been apostles longer so that people would talk about them and they could write the Gospels. Of course, it's amusing to the audience who knows that we will, in fact, talk about them and read their Gospels.[2]

We will know them as the 12 ordinary men Jesus chose to do extraordinary things. They had no ordination certificate or even an extra shirt. Yet they were given Jesus' authority to heal, cast out demons, and raise the dead!

Why do you think Jesus would call ordinary and even flawed people to be his disciples?

. . . Anyone Can Do It

Wait a minute! Raise the dead?!

Keep in mind that the New Testament records accounts of others besides Jesus who rose from the dead. Matthew tells how Jesus raised Jairus's daughter (Matthew 9:18-26) and about the many holy people who came out of their graves and went into Jerusalem after Jesus was resurrected (27:52-53). And John tells us the story of the raising of Lazarus (John 11:1-44).

But there were also at least two occasions when the power to raise the dead was exercised by an apostle: Eutychus was raised by the agency of Paul (Acts 20:9-12) and Tabitha through the agency of Peter (Acts 9:36-42).

Jesus' resurrection power was on the move! Wherever Jesus went, death was under threat.

Now, if the authority to raise the dead seems impossible, then the authority to heal and to cast out demons seems only slightly less impossible. Sure, we can point to the advances in modern medicine and psychiatric science and say, "They just didn't understand illness back then like we do now." But let us not try too hard to wedge this text into a modern category and miss out on its power.

Even if you have trouble getting your imagination around stories of healing and the casting out of demons, consider how the world is far from how God would have it to be. Consider the grip that evil has on the systems that affect our lives and on our imaginations. Thus the power of the passage is in how Jesus actually gave his disciples radical authority to be part of the cosmos-changing work Christ is doing in the world!

Barbara Brown Taylor imagines being among the disciples when Jesus bestowed his authority on them: "He holds his big hands out over your heads and says a prayer that travels down your backbone like a chill, giving you authority over demons, over disease—even over death."[3]

Can you imagine it too? Pray that you can and will. For you are a disciple of Jesus Christ! You have been given authority!

Yes, that mission includes ordinary tasks such as washing hundreds of tiny Communion cups or organizing the choir's sheet music. But it also includes the extraordinary and unexplainable works of Christ in the world!

Where have you seen Jesus at work in our world to heal, cast out, and overcome death?

. . . *You Can Do It*

So now you feel ready to go out and do all that Jesus did, right? I'm guessing no. If it were that simple, we'd be living in a dramatically different world right now.

Preacher and professor Thomas G. Long says that we're not, in fact, meant to try to do the very same mighty deeds Jesus did now that he is gone. "The point, rather, is that God, who was at work in the world in Jesus, is still at work in the world in Christ. Wherever there is disease, evil, hope, unbelief, and death, Christ the merciful savior is at work to proclaim the gospel of hope, to heal people from every disease, to cast out the demonic forces of evil, to defeat the ruthless grip of death."[4] We are not to replace Jesus. Rather, we are to join Christ in his work in the world.

But something still holds us back. Maybe we don't want to develop an oversized sense of self. Authority? Healing? Me? Surely Jesus meant someone else.

But Jesus put it clearly several verses later: "Disciples aren't greater than their teacher"; rather, "it's enough for disciples to be like their teacher" (Matthew 10:24, 25). Just because we seek to be like Jesus doesn't mean we are trying to supplant him. In fact, we are accountable to him for what we've done in his name (Romans 14:12).

So what else might hold us back from accepting the authority Jesus gives? What else gets in the way? An insecurity perhaps? a fear of rejection?

Such a fear is realistic. Jesus himself knew what it was to be rejected. Remember just a couple chapters back in Matthew when Jesus cast demons out of two men and sent them into a herd of pigs? The whole herd of pigs rushed down a cliff and over into a lake where they drowned. "Then the whole city came out and met Jesus. When they saw him, they pleaded with him to leave their region" (Matthew 8:34). Or who can forget Jesus' first homecoming sermon in Nazareth?

He was the featured preacher. Local boy made good. The sermon was brief and to the point, but the locals weren't so sure they liked Jesus after all when he said that he was the fulfillment of the prophecies of Isaiah. When Jesus then criticized them, they tried to throw him off a cliff, "but he passed through the crowd and went on his way" (Luke 4:30).

So Jesus certainly knew rejection. He even quoted Psalm 118 himself when he said, *"The stone that the builders rejected has become the cornerstone"* (Matthew 21:42). And Jesus' Passion and Crucifixion was, of course, the world's great rejection of him.

Perhaps that's why he went on to teach his disciples what to do when they were rejected. "If anyone refuses to welcome you or listen to your words, shake the dust off your feet as you leave that house or city" (10:14).

In Jesus' time, when an observant Jew traveled into the Gentile territories, they might be seen to dust off their feet before walking back into the Promised Land. So this action was familiar to Jesus' first hearers. Here Jesus was applying the dust-shaking practice on a household-by-household level. Some houses would be "worthy." Jesus said to give them "your blessing of peace" (verse 13). But if "anyone refuses to welcome you or listen to your words," Jesus said, "shake the dust off your feet as you leave that house or city" (verse 14).

Think about the dust for a moment. Sam Wells once connected the dust from our feet to the dust of Genesis 2 when God made Adam from the dust. And again to Genesis 3:19, where God told Adam, "You are dust, and to dust you shall return" (NRSV). Can you make anything with dust? Not really. Can God? Absolutely![5]

So when we are worried about rejection, we do well to remember that not everyone was pleased to hear from Jesus either. And Jesus knows that not everyone will want to hear about him from us.

But as Jesus told his disciples, he was sending them as "sheep among wolves" (Matthew 10:16). But Jesus said they shouldn't worry. The Spirit of God would give them the words to speak. "Whoever stands firm in the end will be saved" (verse 22). These promises prefigure the ones at the end of the Gospel when Jesus said, "I've received all authority in heaven and on earth," and "I myself will be with you every day until the end of this present age" (28:18, 20).

What a far cry all of this is from most of our church culture in North America. It's a challenge for some churches even to accept someone in their midst who doesn't look or act like them. Going out and being rejected? Even being persecuted or killed? Unfathomable.

But Jesus saw the crowds, and he had compassion on them "because they were troubled and helpless, like sheep without a shepherd" (9:36). He told his followers to pray for "the Lord of the harvest to send out workers for his harvest" (9:38). Little did the disciples know that they would become the answer to their own prayer.[6]

Now we are the answer to that prayer, and we are to have confidence in Jesus who gives great authority. Jesus encourages us as we go about this urgent work. What we do in Jesus' name counts in the kingdom of God!

Imagine walking with Jesus from house to house in your neighborhood. Where would Jesus take you? Where would he want you to go?

Lord of the harvest, send laborers into your vineyard. Number me among them. Grant that I may accept your authority to proclaim the nearness of your kingdom without fear; in Jesus' name I pray. Amen.

1. From "The Unqualified Twelve," by Beverly R. Gaventa in *The Christian Century*, Volume 110, Number 17 (May 19-26, 1993); page 549.
2. From "The Unqualified Twelve"; page 549.
3. From *Bread of Angels*, by Barbara Brown Taylor (Lanham, Maryland: Rowman & Littlefield Publishers, Inc., 1997); page 155.
4. From *Matthew (Westminster Bible Companion)*; by Thomas G. Long (Louisville, Kentucky: Westminster John Knox Press, 1997); page 117.
5. From "Shaking the Dust," by Samuel Wells for FaithAndLeadership.com (2013) (faithandleadership.com/samuel-wells-shaking-dust).
6. From *Matthew (Westminster Bible Companion)*; page 114.

MONDAY
Jeremiah 1:4-10

"I'm only a child." That seems like a perfectly reasonable objection to being called to serve the Lord as a prophet. How old was Jeremiah when God called him? Who knows? In the ancient world, boys in Jewish tradition became men at age 12. Some surrounding cultures began training children for war at age 6. As for whether Jeremiah was under the age of 12, though, we don't know. He could have just felt too young to do the work ahead of him.

Perhaps you have felt the same way before. Perhaps you have been charged with a responsibility that seemed far beyond your years.

Because of a bizarre confluence of events, I ended up being the person who told my grandmother that my grandfather had passed away. I was 10. Believe me, when that mantle passed to me, I was saying to whomever would listen (which turned out to be no one), "Hey, I am only a child!" So what? There was a job to do that had to be done. Buck up and deal. That's what I had to do, and that is what Jeremiah had to do too.

Jeremiah was called to be the prophet to the nations! Seriously, God? Why do you do this to us? Why do you see so much more potential in us than we want you to see?

Anyway, as the prophet to the nations, Jeremiah was going to spend the bulk of his career trying to get the Southern Kingdom of Judah to yoke itself to Babylon. Nobody, *nobody* (including at times Jeremiah) thought that was a good idea. Everyone except Jeremiah was pretty sure that was not the will of God, so they didn't yoke themselves to Babylon. They were slaughtered and hauled into exile.

Jeremiah was not a popular guy with his own people, and what he was saying seemed contrary to how the people of God understood themselves. But he was still right.

Is there someone in your church who is a good and loving person but who regularly tells the church that you need to do something differently? Are you dismissing her or him? Maybe, just maybe, you should stop and listen.

The reality is, the church is becoming more and more marginalized. We are going to have to pay more attention to the culture and circumstances around us. We may have to make some radical changes in order to reach more people for Jesus. In fact, that may be God's exact will for us.

But how do we know what is the right thing to do? We will know because God is still raising up prophets to the nations. Prophets who are fluent in pop culture and millennial identity. Prophets who also love God and the church. But to hear their message, we have to stop and listen. Stop. And listen.

Lord Jesus, help me to hear your prophets, then and now. Amen.

TUESDAY

Acts 9:10-19

Yesterday's reading from Jeremiah led us to look at the difficulty of being called to deliver bad news to our own people. Now imagine being called to go help the man who is participating in the effort to have you arrested—or killed!

This Ananias is one of the unsung heroes of the Bible. He did something incredibly brave in approaching Saul. Sure, Jesus showed up and told him that was what he should do, but come on!

What Ananias did was to take seriously two key teachings of Jesus. The first is, "Love your enemies and pray for those who harass you" (Matthew 5:44). We see Ananias show love in the first place because he showed up, but in the second place because he called Saul a brother (Acts 9:17).

Brother is a term of inclusion, of assuming that Saul was already part of the family of Jesus' followers, even when Ananias had no concrete evidence that was the case. He was willing ahead of time to extend tremendous love and hospitality.

Then, Ananias touched Saul and prayed for his healing. If Saul remained blind, he would no longer be a threat. There was little purpose for a blind person in the Greco-Roman world. If he was healed and he was still bent on arresting Christ-followers, then Ananias had effectively handed himself over. Yet he prayed for this man's healing anyway.

The second key teaching that Ananias adhered to is the

108

Great Commission: Go and make disciples and baptize them (Matthew 28:19). As soon as Saul was healed, someone, presumably Ananias, baptized Saul immediately. Was Saul's conversion authentic, or was it a ruse to get close to the believers? Ananias's only proof that it was authentic was that Jesus had said this was the way it would be.

I know I don't trust Jesus like that all the time. I would like to think that in a moment like this, I would come through for Jesus, but would I? Would you? But where would Christianity be without Saul/Paul, our greatest evangelist ever?

This story speaks an uncomfortable truth to us. All too often, we do not seek out people who are significantly different from us because we view them as threats. With whose eyes are we seeing these people? Certainly not Jesus' eyes. Jesus sees the potential in everyone.

When we look at the surface, or when we allow fear to rule our hearts, we do damage to God's kingdom. We miss an opportunity to help someone live a life dedicated to Jesus. It is possible that stain will remain on our hands. We have to start opening ourselves up to God's possibilities. How many Sauls have we already missed because we were not ready and willing like Ananias?

Jesus, encourage me to do the work to prepare my heart to love my enemy and to be willing to bring anyone to the faith. Amen.

WEDNESDAY

Acts 16:6-10

Whenever I study Acts with others, someone invariably asks, "Why couldn't Paul and his companions go to Asia?" I always have the same answer: "I don't know. God told them not to go!" I hate to default to the "Because God said so!" answer, but what am I supposed to do? The text doesn't give us much to work with there. Maybe God knew they would face hurdles too great, or maybe God had other plans for how the good news would go there.

I understand the curiosity around such a strange detail. We find a number of gaps in the Bible that we would like to have filled. Those gaps do inspire us to tap into our creative brains though and imagine what was happening there, maybe better than if we had more intricate detail. And speaking of those brains. . . .

Paul was called away to Macedonia by the vision of a man. This was not the first vision to direct Paul. When he encountered the voice of Christ on the road to Damascus, he was blinded. Following that blinding, at some point he received a vision that a man named Ananias would come and cure his blindness. Later, in Corinth, Paul also received a vision in which the Lord encouraged him to keep speaking and not be afraid (Acts 18:9).

Visions seem to be an important means of communication in the Book of Acts. What is interesting about Paul's visions is that he saw people other than the Lord or the Lord's angel in his. This was in contrast to Ananias, Peter, and Cornelius who all saw the Lord (or the Lord's angel/messenger) in their visions. Paul's first vision was of Ananias curing him (9:12), while his second one was of a Macedonian man (16:9). It was not until Paul was in Corinth under threat that he had a vision of the Lord telling him to keep speaking and not be afraid (18:9).

Paul's prior interactions with God had been with the voice of Christ, not in a vision, and with the Holy Spirit or the Spirit of Jesus as recounted in this passage, but again, not specifically in a vision. Does this mean Paul needed to work up to seeing the Lord/the Lord's angel in a vision? Was there still a bit of disbelief in Paul that made a vision of the Lord a problem? Or was it the reverse: that Paul was now so in tune with the will of God that he could see other people as God saw them, hearing their prayers across miles and seeing them in his visions, and he only needed a vision of the Lord when his courage began to falter?

Paul seemed so assured in his call and belief that the latter possibility makes more sense to me. Regardless, what we do learn from Paul's story is that God will use any number of ways to communicate to us God's will for us. We just have to be open to receiving such a word.

Lord, help me be open to all the ways you are speaking to me, and let me listen with an open heart. Amen.

THURSDAY

Mark 6:7-13

By the time you read this, I will be the mother of a 16-year-old. Now, I cannot guarantee you he will be driving yet, because many in this generation are just not interested in such things. But he could be. Which means there will have been a day when I handed keys over to him, giving him authority over a potentially lethal machine.

I will have given him provisions so he won't have to ask for gas money from anyone else because he will have enough to get home. I will have expected him to drive safely and use the car only for getting from Point A to Point B. I will have to trust that everything I have ever taught him will serve him well.

I think I know how Jesus felt.

Imagine giving a group of ragtag fishermen and tax collectors "*authority over unclean spirits*" (Mark 6:7; italics added)! Giving them all this power and then sending them out with minimal provisions, trusting not only that they would return but also that they would remember all he taught them and use it well.

I wonder what it was like for Jesus in the days before they came home. I wonder what it is like for Jesus every single day.

Isn't that what Jesus does every day? Jesus sends disciples out into the world, people representing his name, with access to the greatest power in the universe, every single day. What do we do with it?

A lot of bad things. Some people use that power to condemn

others, to degrade and humiliate other people made in the image of God. To strip the earth of all its resources without regard to the future because we were given authority over the earth. Some people even kill in the name of Jesus.

A lot of nothing. Some of us do not believe there is real power in the name of Jesus, and so we do nothing in his name. What is the point? We don't think it will change anything.

And a lot of good things. Some of us use that power to set others free, to show love to everyone we meet. To protect the earth and the vulnerable among us. To help people trapped by demons beat them back into submission. Some of us even give our lives in the name of Jesus. At one point, Jesus described himself as longing to be like a mother hen who gathers the faithful under her wings (Luke 13:34). This moment, though, is when the mother hen encourages the chicks to spread their wings and try to fly.

And these chicks cast out demons and healed people. They made Jesus proud.

Will I? Will you? Take thou authority, and let's go find out.

Protective and empowering Jesus, help me make you proud. Amen.

FRIDAY

Matthew 9:35-38

When I was a pastor in West Memphis, Arkansas, I made it a point to experience a different crop harvest every year. The first year, I rode on the combines for the soybean harvest. I sat in a million-dollar machine that had the field GPS mapped into it. The farmer told the combine which row to cut, and it drove itself there and started cutting.

This mass of plants and dirt and weeds all got drawn into the blades. But as I turned around, in the bay behind me I saw only beans, perfectly shelled already. Then, as the bay filled, a transport truck pulled up beside us. While the combine kept cutting a row, a shaft extended from our machine over the back of the truck, and it shot the beans from us to them. The whole operation took two people. I was the third, but I was just along for the ride.

The second year, I went out for the cotton harvest. They also had their own machines that did the majority of cutting the field, but there were far more workers in the field. Cotton, it turns out, is a bit more of a hands-on crop. They had to load it into a big baler. But, then, in addition to putting metal plates on it to push the cotton down, it was still more effective to have people stomping on the cotton to pack it down tight and make sure there was as little loss as possible. It took a crowd to get it done.

Jesus must have felt like a cotton farmer fighting a soybean industry for help. He could look up and see the well-oiled, million-dinar machine of the Temple. One priest at a time would go into the Holy of Holies to get the job done, and only on certain days. Even so, there was far more than just one priest working there. But in the meantime, there was a sea of people outside the Temple, desperately in need of personal attention; but everyone wanted to work in the other field. "Shiny" was beating out "down in the dirt" hands down.

Discipleship is something like picking cotton. It cannot be handed off to a machine. It cannot be the business of big business, even if that big business comes disguised with a steeple on top. Discipleship, and bringing others to the faith, is the work of one-on-one relationships. It takes all hands on deck to make sure no one gets lost under the pressure of life.

When we give discipleship its due attention though, including especially evangelizing and cultivating new workers in the field, we weave something beautiful. We weave the fabric of our lives: a strong, sound faith in Jesus Christ.

Jesus, cultivate your love in me so that I may plant that love in others. Amen.

SATURDAY

Matthew 10:16-25

It is not hard to be a Christian in the United States. We may not enjoy the prominence we once did; but let's be honest, that prominence also meant we watered down Jesus' radical message of love to be palatable to more people.

We do live in Post-Christendom, which means that we are in an era and a culture that no longer centers around Christianity. It is not, by the way, the same in the Southern hemisphere where Christianity is growing by leaps and bounds. Here in the northern half of the world, we do have work to do. But my life is not under threat when I stand up on Sundays and preach from the pulpit.

There are Christians around the world, however, who are under threat. There are places in Africa and Asia where Christianity is illegal. Practicing your faith could result in fines, imprisonment, and perhaps even death.

The first Christians lived in what is now modern-day Israel-Palestine. Today, in the midst of tense and often violent conflict between Muslims and Jews, Christians in that area are getting crushed. They have absolutely no power. They lose land and have restricted access of travel on all sides of the conflict. Christians now make up only 2 percent of the population in Israel and 4 percent of the population in the Middle East.[1] In our rush to support Israel or defend Palestinian Muslims, somehow we have forgotten to take notice of the Christians caught in the conflict; and they are being systematically rooted out of our spiritual homeland.

It is not terribly different than the reality in which the apostles found themselves in the first century. Caught between two dominant forces, Israel and Rome, Christians would find themselves persecuted on all sides. Jesus knew this was coming. He knew that not only would there be political persecution, but families would persecute family members.

Into this terrible situation, Jesus gave them words of comfort. First, he told them to keep their wits about them (wise as snakes) but also to respond naively (innocent as doves). To watch out for people but also to continue delivering his message to those same people, which they would be able to do because the Spirit would give them the words.

Ultimately, he reminded them that what they would go through, he would have already gone through. They would not be alone. He would be with them to strengthen them. And he would know, more than anyone, exactly how they felt. Praise God for Jesus the Christ!

Lord Jesus, we lift up all the Christians around the world who are experiencing persecution. May they know your peace. Amen.

1. From pewresearch.org/fact-tank/2016/05/10/5-facts-about-israeli-christians/.

6

A HEART OF EXTRAVAGANT LOVE

The Sixth Sunday in Lent

Matthew 26:1-13

"You have to spend money to make money," the executive director of a charity told me when I asked him why his organization was spending so much on their big gala. I knew he was trying to attract donors who had an excess of disposable income. But pony rides? A cruise ship? Pony rides on a cruise ship?! Shouldn't someone say, "Enough is enough! We shouldn't spend this kind of money as a charity!"

Or consider presidential inaugurations. Every four years, taxpayers in the United States foot most of the bill. About $70 million comes from private donations, but the rest comes from the federal government. The overall cost has been steadily rising toward $200 million![1] It's an important ceremony to be sure, but how much is too much?

It's likely that your church has at some point wrestled with decisions about how much to spend to maintain an organ, repair stained glass windows, pay instrumentalists for a cantata, or replace faded paraments. At what point does the expense constitute a "waste"?

Such questions were on the minds of the disciples in Matthew 26:1-13, when an unnamed woman entered a dinner at Simon's house, broke open an alabaster vase of expensive perfume, and poured it over Jesus' head. They said, "Why this waste? This perfume could have been sold for a lot of money and given to the poor" (Matthew 26:8-9). "Why do you make trouble for the woman? She's done a good thing for me," Jesus replied. "By pouring this perfume over my body she's prepared me to be buried" (verses 10, 12).

There it is. A battle between two competing goods. The perfume was a finite resource that could go to serve the poor or used to worship Jesus. To the disciples, these were mutually exclusive options. Who was in the right? The woman or the disciples?

Service?

We know that Jesus answered that question, and we know what his answer was. But if it's at all possible, try to suspend that knowledge for just a moment. Consider the disciples' position (if only to better understand Jesus' point).

Jesus criticized the disciples in this case, but not for their concern for the poor. After all, they had already heard Jesus tell a young man to "go, sell what you own, and give the money to the poor" (Matthew 19:21). In the chapter just preceding this text, we find Jesus saying, "When you have done it for one of the least of these brothers and sisters of mine, you have done it for me" (25:40). Then there were the numerous times Jesus confronted the lures of wealth in his teachings. So the disciples were just applying Jesus' teachings as they understood them. They were "angry," but theirs was a righteous anger (26:8). In the accounts of this story in the Gospels of Mark and John, one or more of the disciples remark that the perfume could have been sold for almost a year's pay (Mark 14:5; John 12:5)! (And what is it they say about an engagement ring? Two months' salary?)

And how did this look to the poor? Remember that this extravagant act wasn't in the lavish courtyard of the high priest Caiaphas in which our text began today. It was at the home of Simon, "who had a skin disease" (Matthew 26:6), which had made him ritualistically unclean. Such a condition likely took him out of work and participation in the local economy. Were the disciples speaking for Simon too?

We don't know for sure. Matthew records no words from Simon or from the anonymous woman. But that didn't stop the disciples from trying to speak on behalf of the poor. They had decided, rightly or wrongly, that this woman couldn't afford to make such a gift to Jesus. And still today those with means have been known to take it upon themselves to decide how the poor should spend their meager resources.

So let's see what Jesus had to say.

How much is "too much" for the church to spend on something that will be used to glorify God? Who should decide such things?

Worship?

Jesus was upset at how the disciples rushed to judge the woman with the alabaster vase. He scolded the disciples: "Why do you make trouble for the woman? She's done a good thing for me" (Matthew 26:10). Jesus recognized that the woman was worshipping him. She was literally pouring her worship upon him. Jesus saw the ethical objection of the disciples as secondary to her worship.

Remember when the legal expert asked Jesus, "What is the greatest commandment in the Law" (22:36)? Jesus replied that love of God is "the first and greatest commandment" (22:38). The second is to "*love your neighbor as you love yourself*" (22:39).

Jesus, who is God's gift to the poor, is more valuable than even a vase of expensive perfume. He is God's answer to a needy world. "All acts of Christian ministry grow out of this one profound act of Jesus' ministry," writes Thomas G. Long.[2]

Just as the unnamed woman poured out her perfume on Jesus, so did Jesus pour out his life for her, for the disciples, and for all of us. I like how Sam Wells paraphrased Jesus' reaction: "Don't you *see*? She's behaving just like me! She's demonstrating the extravagance of human love. She's poured out her whole self—financial, social, emotional—to gain your attention by a gesture of sheer beauty. I'm demonstrating the extravagance of *divine* love. I'm pouring out my whole self, physical, spiritual,

121

metaphysical, to gain your attention by a gesture of sheer beauty. I am the extravagance of God. And if you're taking no notice of *her*, then how much worse that you're taking no notice of *me*."[3]

We need to make an important clarification here about Jesus' remark: "You always have the poor with you, but you won't always have me" (26:11). People commonly use this verse to defend apathy toward the poor. Christians wrongly assume that Jesus was saying, "Don't feel too bad about the poor. There will always be some poor people." Nothing could be further from Jesus' intent.

Jesus was echoing Deuteronomy 15:11 in which God said to Israel, "Poor persons will never disappear from the earth. That's why I'm giving you this command: you must open your hand generously to your fellow Israelites, to the needy among you, and to the poor who live with you in your land."

The poor will always be present to be served by Jesus' disciples. Jesus would not always be present in bodily form. However, Christians have come to know the presence of Christ "where two or three are gathered" in his name and especially among "the least of these" (Matthew 18:20; 25:40).

Lillian Daniels was the pastor of a church in Connecticut with a long history and a grand building that they struggled to fill with worshippers. Like many churches, they had a room they called the parlor that was well-appointed but seldom used. A turning point came when they began to hold lavish teas after worship, not for fancy rich people but for the poor who lived near their downtown building. When people came to the upstairs parlor, they gasped. "Surely this room isn't for us?" they would ask. But it was.

"I look around to see people who do not have this elegance at home enjoy it in community," Daniels recalls. "I see people who have no china of their own get to own the china of the church. People whose usual lunch is a yogurt slurped down while standing in front of the refrigerator get to sit down instead in the parlor, with a lovely plate full of treats. . . . A recent widow who lives alone gets to preside over the pouring of the tea. She sits behind a silver tea service that generations before her have washed, polished, and drunk from. Here she presides over a crowd. As she is pulled out of loneliness, tentatively stepping out for a moment from the shadow of her grief, there at the head table she pours out for others what has already been poured out for her."[4]

What worship practices are, for you, a pouring out of your best for Jesus?

Smells

When John wrote of this event (or one like it), he said, "The house was filled with the aroma of the perfume" (John 12:3). In preaching on this text, I've sometimes put small drops of perfume from the region of Bethany on index cards and put a card at the end of each sanctuary pew. I then tell worshippers to waft the smell in front of them (if they aren't allergic). Together we imagine being in the room with the woman and Jesus as the fragrant perfume was poured out.

Smells are powerful and evocative. We associate people, places, and things with smells. For example, my wife doesn't like the smell of mothballs, but it reminds me of fun visits to my grandparents' homes when I was young. Smells are like that. They connect with us on a deep level.

There was certainly something in the air on that occasion at Simon's house besides the expensive perfume. It was the foreboding smell of things to come. Just two days before the Passover, the chief priests and elders had been "plotting to arrest Jesus by cunning tricks and to kill him" (Matthew 26:4).

After the disciples became upset about the perfume, Judas went right out and betrayed Jesus to the chief priests for 30 pieces of silver (verses 14-15). In John's version, Judas was even the one who complained about the perfume (John 12:4-6). Thus the anonymous woman's act of worship was dramatically bookended by the plot to kill Jesus and Judas' betrayal.

Elizabeth B. Ford explains: "Whereas Matthew portrays the male characters—the chief priests, the disciples, and Judas—in a negative light, the woman emerges as a model of devotion. Their calculating stands in striking contrast to her unmeasured giving."[5]

Her act is all the more striking because it came to Jesus as a respite in the midst of struggle and strain. Perhaps it is for this reason that Jesus praised her and said, "Wherever in the whole world this good news is announced, what she's done will also be told in memory of her" (Matthew 26:13). We are right to wish that Matthew had memorialized her by telling us her name, too. But we honor her and the memory of what she did.

What smells conjure up vivid memories for you? What do you imagine Simon's house smelled like after the perfume was poured upon Jesus?

Worship/Service!

We can honor the generous woman of this text by following her example. She put the worship of Jesus before all else. Seeming to know that he was near the end of his earthly life, she prepared him for burial while he was still alive. (Notice how the women in Matthew's Crucifixion account did not go to anoint Jesus' body after burial? It had already been anointed.)

So often we Christians divide our ministry into two categories: worship and service. Sometimes we are praying; other times we are serving. Some of us prefer to go to worship; others prefer to help at a mission worksite.

But these are false categories. Worship is a form of service. Service is a form of worship. God takes no delight in words not matched with deeds. Neither is God looking for mere "volunteers" for community improvement projects. God calls disciples who worship and serve. These are not mutually exclusive. Might we consider referring to these two as worship/service? By which I do not mean a service-of-worship. Rather, could we blur the distinctions between the two such that we can hardly distinguish one from the other?

I am encouraged by the practices I have seen in some Christian communities in recent years to hold service and worship together and to intentionally blur the lines between them. At the very least, for example, a congregation's work teams can pray together at their mission sites. Their hosts or partners in mission can be welcomed to join the worship if they wish.

Or when the church collects food or clothing or other such

125

goods for local donation, those items can be displayed on the altar table or the Communion rail for a Sunday, reminding us that our acts of service are acts of worship.

In one church I know, the congregation worships in a large, beautiful, downtown sanctuary. But they needed to sit closer to one another and to the front to strengthen congregational singing and to further the bonds of fellowship. What did they do with all the empty pews in the back? They turned them into "mission pews" where they collect items for the shelters, schools, and other mission fields around them.

These are just examples of how worship and service can be intertwined. But the greatest example is Jesus, the object of our worship and the hope of the world.

How might your congregation blur the lines between worship and service?

Anoint me with your grace, Lord Jesus. Give me the will to give you all of my worship. You are worthy of all praise! I pray in the name of Jesus. Amen.

1. From "How Much Does an Inauguration Cost? And Who Pays for What?" by Roxanne Roberts in *The Washington Post* (December 13, 2016).
2. From *Matthew (Westminster Bible Companion)*; page 293.
3. From "A Criminal Waste," a sermon preached by Sam Wells in the Duke University Chapel, Durham, North Carolina, March 14, 2010 (chapel-archives.oit.duke.edu/documents/sermons/March21ACriminalWaste.pdf).
4. From *This Odd and Wondrous Calling*, by Lillian Daniel and Martin B. Copenhaver (William B. Eerdmans Publishing Company, 2009); pages 26-28.
5. From *Interpretation*, by Elizabeth B. Ford, Volume 59, Number 4 (October 2005); page 401.

MONDAY
John 12:1-8

John's Gospel account of Jesus being anointed by a woman gives some specifics that Matthew's Gospel does not.

From this passage, we know that it was Mary who anointed Jesus, unlike in the other Gospels when the woman who anointed Jesus is unnamed. Unfortunately, it was a Mary who anointed him. The reason that is unfortunate is that the Marys in the Gospels tend to get compressed into one another.

There is specifically a long tradition of assuming that Mary Magdalene and Mary of Bethany, sister of Martha and Lazarus, were the same person. Some of this is due to legends about what happened to the Marys after Jesus' resurrection. Some of it is due to one of the popes giving a compelling sermon in which he assumed that Mary of Bethany and Mary Magdalene and the "woman from the city" who anointed Jesus in the Gospel of Luke were all the same person, which is how we also got this tradition that Mary Magdalene was a prostitute, even though the Gospels never say or even imply such a thing.

There is a ready problem with assuming Mary of Bethany and Mary Magdalene were the same person. The reason Mary Magdalene was called Magdalene is because it meant "from Magdala." Magdala was a town on the Sea of Galilee. Bethany was sandwiched between Jerusalem and Bethlehem. Clearly these are different places, and clearly the women were different Marys as well.

Another specific detail that John gives that Matthew does

not is that Mary used nard to anoint Jesus. Nard comes from an herb that grows in the Himalayan region of India. The root and lower stems were dried and then made into an ointment. Then that ointment had to travel thousands of miles to reach the Holy Land, and it went by camel or foot. Imagine the extravagance of that moment: Mary pouring three quarters of a pound of pure nard ointment on Jesus.

No wonder the response of the disciples (here, specifically Judas) was one of derision. When had they ever thought to honor him this way?

Maybe the disciples just assumed that Jesus would always be with them, which is what makes Jesus' response that they would always have the poor, but not always him, that much more poignant.

If I am honest, however, I all too often take Jesus' presence in my life for granted as well. I am sometimes shocked, even offended, when someone who is what I consider to be a church outsider has a far more intimate encounter with Jesus than I do. Perhaps I would do well to more often follow Mary of Bethany's example and pour extravagant love on my Savior.

Beautiful Jesus, help me love you better. Amen.

TUESDAY

John 11:47-53

If you ever want a good, accessible book on different schools of ethics, I recommend *Beyond Bumper Sticker Ethics: An Introduction to the Theories of Right and Wrong* by Steve Wilkens. One of the ethical approaches Wilkens covers is utilitarianism, which states that what is good and right is whatever is good for the most people. In other words, the greatest happiness for the greatest number.

Whether he named it that or not, Caiaphas was using utilitarian ethics. He had any number of ways to argue that killing Jesus, or at least having him put to death by the Roman Empire, would be beneficial to Israel. First, there is the obvious answer that if they stopped his rabble-rousing, the Romans would get off their backs. Here, though, Caiaphas also tied into his own apparently earlier prophecy in which he predicted that Jesus would die so that God's scattered children would be gathered together as one.

I don't think that Caiaphas intended his prophecy to mean that people all over the known world would unite to follow Jesus. He probably thought it would somehow mean a strengthening of Jewish identity and power so that those Jews in the Diaspora could come home. I also don't think that Caiaphas conceived of Jesus as the ultimate sacrifice who would take away the need for the blood sacrifices at the Temple because he would have given his life definitively for all people.

The idea that Jesus sacrificed himself for the good of the many certainly fits within utilitarian ethics. That may work for God to give of God's self that way. But many other teachings of Jesus directly contradict such a notion. For instance, remember the crazed Gerasene man who had to live among the tombs? He was healed but at the cost of a whole herd of pigs for which the swineherds were never compensated (Mark 5:1-17). Or how about the idea that a shepherd leaves his 99 sheep vulnerable to go in search of the one who has wandered off (Luke 15:4-6)?

Before we go using utilitarian ethics when we make decisions, we should stop and ask ourselves, *Is someone lost in this situation?* Because if someone is lost, then we might not be doing what Jesus taught us to do.

Sometimes in the church, taking a vote and following majority rule is the right thing, but sometimes we instead need to listen to that one lone voice who is saying something different than everyone else. If that one voice is paying attention to the most vulnerable and hurting among us, that voice is probably speaking the gospel of Christ. The other may be the words of the Pharisees.

Lord, may we always be attentive to the lost ones around us, and may we recognize when the many must sacrifice for the one. Amen.

WEDNESDAY

Matthew 26:14-16

Judas is a difficult figure to study. Part of that is because the information we have is so sparse. We are never given much insight into why Judas decided to hand Jesus over to the Jewish authorities. In Luke and John, we are told it is because Satan entered into him. Matthew's portrayal is more ambiguous. Let's look at this point when he decided to make a deal with the chief priests.

First, let's consider Judas's name. Judas's first name was incredibly common at the time. In fact, arguably three of the disciples may have had that same first name, but two of them, Thaddaeus and Thomas, may have gone by nicknames to keep things clear. Jesus also seems to have had a brother named Judas (Matthew 13:55). Like the name *Adolf* following World War II, however, the popularity of the name *Judas* would drop off sharply, in Christian circles especially.

His last name, however, seems to be a bit of a mystery. *Iscariot* is not a usual last name for the time. It sounds like *sikarios*. *Sikarios* means "assassin" or "betrayer." It may, then, not have been his true last name at all, but instead marked him as one who betrayed Jesus.

Or perhaps it means that Judas had ties to the *sicarii*. The *sicarii* were a splinter group of Jewish zealots who tended to assassinate Romans or Hebrews sympathetic to Romans. If Judas was a revolutionary, he may have seen in Jesus someone who could overthrow the Roman Empire.

131

Consider when Judas decided to turn Jesus in right after the woman had anointed Jesus, and Jesus had said it was for his death. Perhaps Judas was tired of Jesus talking about dying. Judas had seen the powerful things Jesus could do. Maybe Judas had more faith in Jesus than anyone. Maybe Judas assumed that if Jesus was put in a tough position, or if he was brought before a high enough Roman official, that he would use his miraculous powers to overthrow Rome and restore Israel.

But what about the 30 pieces of silver? Why did he want the money if his aims were purely revolutionary? Maybe he was greedy. Or perhaps he knew it would look too suspicious to just agree to hand over Jesus for nothing. After all, we will see that when Jesus was condemned to death, Judas tried to return the money. That was not an act of greed but remorse. We cannot know the motivations behind Judas's actions because we do not know his whole story. It makes me wonder, Have I ever unfairly judged someone based on how that person is portrayed, especially if that portrayal comes from people who hate them? I am sure I have.

Lord Jesus, help me to listen to the whole of the story and to seek forgiveness for all, including me. Amen.

MAUNDY THURSDAY

Matthew 26:17-29

The last Passover meal. Was it? In one sense, yes; in another, no. It was not the last time ever a Passover meal was shared. Jews today still observe the Seder, the modern representation of the Passover meal. This was, however, the last time these disciples and Jesus would sit down to a Passover meal. What would happen in the course of that meal is that this long-honored tradition would transform into another meal of significance: Communion.

Communion would come to be a meal that is observed more often than the once-a-year practice of Passover. The two meals would diverge sharply over the course of time. The sacrificial lamb, however, continues to be represented in the bread and the wine, which for Christians represent the body and blood of the Lamb of God, Jesus Christ.

Would the disciples have grasped the significance of these moments at the time? Perhaps it was not until after the death and resurrection of Jesus that this moment carried a different weight than it did that night. No doubt, as observant Jews, it carried a deep meaning. But could they have predicted that the meaning would shift so dramatically within a few hours?

Meals, and gatherings in general, do change. They change with the addition and subtraction of people in our lives. When we lose someone we love, someone who has been at our table in a significant way, the meals we shared with them change too.

Often, however, we find ways to include them anyway. Think of some of the cultural practices that do this. I visited Mexico during Day of the Dead one year. All around Monterrey, people had built shrines to loved ones; and at the vast majority of those shrines, there were meals that the person loved. It's similar to the inner-city practice of pouring a shot of liquor on the ground in honor of someone who has died, possibly under violent circumstances.

Some families continue to do something to celebrate birthdays of people who have passed away. Widows and widowers may go out for their anniversaries and even sometimes order a meal for their spouses. These are rituals that keep people in our lives. There is something about meals that makes them ripe for ritual.

It is no accident that the Communion meal is so important to us. For the disciples, it became a way to remember an incredibly significant moment in their journey with Jesus. For us, it is the only way we have ever consistently eaten with Jesus. For all of us, it points us to the heavenly banquet we will share with all the ones we love again one day. What a holy time! What a precious place!

Precious Jesus, let me always keep before me the ones I love. Amen.

GOOD FRIDAY
Matthew 27:32-44

Each of the Gospels tells the story of Jesus' crucifixion in a slightly different way. John tells a story of Jesus' exaltation. Luke focuses on how Jesus' journey was a prophetic action and includes the weeping women and a conversation with the two criminals on either side of Jesus. Matthew's and Mark's accounts are close, with Matthew focusing slightly more on the miraculous elements surrounding the Crucifixion, such as the earthquake and the raising of the dead.

Matthew's and Mark's accounts read like a quick play-by-play of the Crucifixion. Events move at an almost breathless pace, just a sparse accounting of action to action. Jesus is barely given a voice, only recounted as quoting Psalm 22. The text reads almost matter-of-factly, which makes the account all the more disturbing. Where is the emotion? Where is the aching? Where is the tragedy?

It felt very much the same for me when I visited the traditional location of Jesus' crucifixion and burial in the Church of the Holy Sepulchre in Jerusalem. I went in the off-season when Israel and Syria were lobbing missiles at each other, so tourism was significantly down. This meant we were able to go into areas that many tour groups do not have time to see.

Still, there was a schedule to keep, so we spent only a few minutes at the location where Jesus was supposedly crucified since we wanted to see other parts of that massive church. There was a short line to go into the supposed tomb location. A guard stationed there timed how long visitors were in there, and we were only allowed about a minute before we were shuffled out for the next group of pilgrims.

It strikes me now that the Crucifixion must have felt routine to the Roman soldiers. It was just their job to nail people to crosses and guard them until they were dead. Just another day at the office. As for the Jewish leaders who campaigned for Jesus' death, this was also one more thing they could check off their list before going about their business. It was only those who had followed and loved Jesus who felt the weight of the day.

On this Good Friday, what are your feelings? Is it just a day off from school or work? Will you go to a special church service, or will you not even give it a passing thought? Is the weight of the Crucifixion on our shoulders, or will it be just another Friday night? Will we recount the story matter-of-factly, or will we hear it and let it shake our world?

Lord Jesus, you gave your all for me. Help me remember and feel the depth of that sacrifice for my soul. Amen.

SATURDAY

John 11:17-27

The Gospel of John records seven "I Am" statements Jesus made:

- I am the Bread of Life (6:35)
- I am the Light of the World (8:12)
- I am the Gate (10:9)
- I am the Good Shepherd (10:11)
- I am the Resurrection and the Life (11:25)
- I am the Way, the Truth, and the Life (14:6)
- I am the Vine (15:5)

When Jesus spoke each of these words, there were things around him that would allow him to make himself clearly real for the people who heard him. He had just fed the multitudes when he told people he is the bread of life. Shepherds, sheepfolds, and vineyards were all around, providing more examples.

Light is a universal experience, as even those who cannot see can feel the warmth of light. Each time people encountered the things Jesus compared himself to, they would be able to remember him. Even in his absence, which he knew was coming, he would continue to be a concrete, material reality to them.

When it comes to the "I Am" statement in this passage, Jesus was preparing to raise Lazarus from the dead. Unlike the other "I Am" statements, which had been largely metaphorical, this one would be literal. Jesus would actually be the life that resurrected Lazarus.

There is potentially an eighth "I Am" statement, but it is grammatically different from the others. "Before Abraham was, I Am" (8:58). This statement recalls the earlier "I Am" claims of the Lord, such as when Moses asked for God's name and God answered, "I Am Who I Am" (Exodus 3:14).

The cumulative effect of Jesus' "I Am" statements in the Gospel of John is to claim that Jesus is in fact God. Then, each of these statements tells us something about God. Jesus as God provides sustenance, warms us and gives us vision, protects, nurtures, guides, connects, and gives eternal life.

Not only do these seven or eight statements remind us of Jesus as incarnate human, they remind us of who God is through Jesus. So the people of the first century looked at a sheepfold on a hill, and they knew God was with them.

If Jesus were with us in human form today, what images might he use to remind us that God is with us every day? Would he use the internet to represent God's infinite knowledge or Google as the source of all answers? Would he use a reliable sedan to represent how God carries us through life?

Whatever he might use, it would need to be readily available and relatable to the majority of people because God seeks to be alive, present, and integral to our everyday lives.

Even as we wait in symbolical darkness on this Holy Saturday, we know that tomorrow we celebrate the Light of the World and the reality of God's presence with us.

Lord Jesus, You Are. Amen.

7

A JOYFUL HEART

Easter Sunday

Matthew 28:1-15

Happy Day of Resurrection! Whether you are reading this for Sunday school on Easter Sunday or another day, I greet you with the good news of the resurrection of Jesus the Christ!

Jim Harnish, retired senior pastor of Hyde Park United Methodist Church in Tampa, Florida, has told a story about a pastor who was waiting outside the delivery room with the family while one of his church members was giving birth to her new baby boy. He knew that if you were in the vicinity of a birthing room, you were bound to hear birthing mothers hollering and even cursing as they underwent the pain of childbirth.

But, to his amazement, this one mother from his congregation kept yelling, "Joy! Joy! Joy!" He was inspired! She was so moved by the beauty of bringing new life into the world that she was overcome with joy and it's all she could say: "Joy! Joy! Jooooy!" Perhaps, he wondered, all of those years of preaching to her and leading her family spiritually had led to her being such a mature disciple of Jesus that she couldn't even feel the pain because she was so overcome with joy. A couple of hours later, the family and friends began visiting the mother's room to see her and the baby. The pastor went in and told her how inspired he was by her outbursts of "Joy! Joy!" She laughed and said to him, "Oh, pastor. I wish that were true." She said, "I wasn't screaming with Joy, I was screaming at Joy. Joy is the name of the midwife."[1]

Easter is the same way, isn't it? It's wonderful and joyous, and we do say—in our hearts and on our lips—"Joy! Joy!" But it's also scary in a way because new life is loosed on the world, and that changes everything. All the categories we used before the Resurrection are shattered. Everything we thought we knew about how the world works is tossed out the window when the Resurrection comes.

That's scary and wonderful.

In Matthew's Resurrection account, Mary Magdalene and another Mary (some believe the mother of Jesus) were on their way "to look at the tomb" (Matthew 28:1). Matthew doesn't say they took spices with them to anoint Jesus' body as in Mark 16:1 or Luke 24:1. For as we read in Matthew 26:12, an unnamed woman had already anointed him for burial.

When the women arrived at the tomb, they were greeted

by an unnamed angel who brought with him an earthquake. Reminiscent of Daniel 7:9, Matthew explains: "His face was like lightning and his clothes as white as snow" (Matthew 28:3). He rolled the stone back for them to see that the tomb was empty! Then he sat on the stone as he addressed them.

Guards were already there keeping watch over the tomb because the chief priests were concerned that Jesus' disciples might come and steal his body and then tell the people, "He's been raised from the dead" (27:64). But when the angel arrived and the earth shook, the guards "shook with fear and became like dead men" (28:4). The irony! The guards who were supposed to frighten off any of Jesus' disciples were themselves scared (almost) to death—and that's after the second earthquake in three days. These were scary times!

However, the angel spoke three important messages to the women: Don't be afraid. He isn't here. Go and tell. These three instructions are still given to us today as Easter people: Don't be afraid. He isn't here. Go and tell.[2]

Don't Be Afraid

Some Bible passages sound so strong in the old King James Version. "Be not afraid" is one of them. It sounds so authoritative: "Be not afraid." But then I imagine a wondrous, beatific, otherworldly being looking at me with his face like lightning and his clothes whiter than snow (Matthew 28:3) and saying, "Be not afraid."

I would still be afraid!

"Don't be afraid" sounds less commanding and more

comforting (verse 5). Mary Magdalene and the other Mary needed comfort when they encountered this bright and shiny angel of the Lord.

It seems like two kinds of fear were present on this occasion: the guards' fear and the women's fear. All of them were frightened by the dazzling supernatural angel. But the guards were also scared of what the chief priests and the governor would do to them if Jesus' body didn't stay in the tomb.

However, the women felt "great fear" and "excitement" (verse 8). Passages like Psalm 34:11 remind us that the fear of the Lord is an appropriate response to God (see especially translations such as NIV and NRSV). Faithful figures of the Bible feared the Lord and often heard an angel tell them, "Don't be afraid."

It's possible to be faithful witnesses to the Resurrection while still maintaining a fear of the Lord. We are right to be in great awe of Resurrection power. After all, death has been overcome! And if you can't count on things like death and taxes, what in the world can you count on?

What range of feelings does the resurrection of Jesus evoke in you?

He Isn't Here

The message from the angel was, "He isn't here, because he's been raised from the dead, just as he said" (Matthew 28:6). "He isn't here" is a proclamation of the Resurrection. So much of the gospel message is summarized in those few words: "He isn't here."

"Here the angel speaks with the knowledge and authority of God," Paul S. Minear has stated. "This is an announcement that no human being could make; the act of resurrection is something that no person is able to witness. So an angel brings the decisive word, thus protecting God from the prying gaze of human beings yet conveying to chosen witnesses an understanding of meanings hidden behind events."[3]

Our text implies that Jesus had already left the tomb when the angel arrived: "because he's been raised from the dead" (verse 6). Scholars refer to this phrasing as the "divine passive." That means an action is taken by an unmentioned force, and the implication is that God did it. "He's been raised from the dead" (verse 6).

Notice that this phrase is also in past tense. Jesus had already been raised. The angel didn't roll the stone away so Jesus could come out. He rolled it away so the women could see that the tomb was empty. "Come, see the place where they laid him," the angel said (verse 6).

Yet the Resurrection event itself actually goes undescribed. Matthew doesn't tell us how Jesus came back to life, how he came out of the tomb, or any other such details. Perhaps Matthew decided to retain the mystery of that moment.

I'm reminded of the various times when babies were born to mothers in my congregation. I love to go see the family and perhaps even hold the new baby. But when I get home, my wife excitedly asks all kinds of good questions: What was her birth weight? How long is she? What time was she born?

To her frustration, I honestly and sheepishly answer, "I

didn't think to ask." Part of me wants to say to her, "Well, the Gospel writers didn't tell us such things about Jesus' birth." But then, I think better of it.

So it is that Matthew didn't give us a moment-by-moment account of the Resurrection. Rather, the account is that the tomb was empty. Jesus was not there. He's been raised from the dead.

"Now hurry, go and tell his disciples" (verse 7).

What helps you believe in the resurrection of Jesus? Information? proof? testimony? faith?

Go and Tell

Off they went "with great fear and excitement" to tell the disciples (Matthew 28:8). They were the first human evangelists after the Resurrection. But along the way, they encountered the risen Jesus!

E. Carson Brisson writes, "His appearance seems deliberately understated in comparison to that of the divine messenger. The earth does not shake. His face does not shine. His clothes do not glitter. He performs no superhuman feats."[4]

Now they've not just seen the angel and the empty tomb. They've seen Jesus himself! Not only did they see him, but they also touched him. "They came and grabbed his feet and worshipped him" (verse 9). Had their fear subsided?

The two Marys prostrated themselves at Jesus' feet like the Magi did in Matthew 2. Their gifts were not gold, frankincense, and myrrh. Rather, they gave him their worship and devotion.

After greeting the two women warmly, Jesus gave them much the same message that the angel gave. "Don't be afraid," he said. "Go and tell" (verse 10).

The good news of the Resurrection must be told. It is not a secret. It's not just a major news flash. It's even bigger than an earthquake. Jesus has been raised! Go and tell!

Go where? Go to Galilee. That's where Jesus carried out his ministry of teaching, healing, and more. Jerusalem was behind him now. He was going back to his disciples whom he now called brothers. "They will see me there" (verse 10). He was on his way to them as he is to us all after Easter.

We can assume that the women did go and tell. Jesus met the disciples on a mountain in Galilee according to Matthew 28:16-20. But first, Matthew draws our attention to some of the guards who went in a different direction.

The women and the guards saw the angel. But while the women went to Galilee to tell the disciples the good news, the guards went back to Jerusalem to tell the chief priests the bad (to them) news.

After meeting with some elders, the priests concocted a story that they wanted the soldiers to tell: "Say that Jesus' disciples came at night and stole his body while you were sleeping" (verse 13). Along with the alibi, the soldiers received "a large sum of money" (verse 12) reminiscent of the 30 pieces of silver the priests paid Judas (26:15). Eugene Boring has noted, "As in the case with Judas, money oils the wheels of hypocrisy—but here the sum is greater. It costs more to suppress the resurrection message than to engineer the crucifixion."[5]

But what if Pilate heard this concocted explanation? The soldiers would be in big trouble. They would be judged as inept for letting Jesus' disciples get past them to steal the body. But if they said that they fell asleep on the job, they would be punished for being lazy. "We will take care of it with him so you will have nothing to worry about," the priests assured the guards (28:14). Perhaps the priests were confident that Pilate could be bought off, too.

At this point in the story we find two competing narratives: Jesus rose from the dead, or his disciples stole his body from the tomb. Matthew says, "This report has spread throughout all Judea to this very day" (verse 15). Other ancient historians have taken note of that rumor as well.[6]

But these are not equally credible stories. "The Gospel's explanation for the empty tomb is presented with the sure authority of an 'angel of the Lord,'" writes Donald Senior, "whereas the story that Jesus' dead body was stolen by the disciples is concocted by discredited religious leaders."[7]

Bishop William H. Willimon has noticed how many moderns are skeptical of the message of Resurrection: "It is hard to believe that there was a time when you had to pay people to disbelieve in the resurrection. Nowadays, disbelief in resurrection is the official position of nearly everyone."[8]

Never underestimate the human proclivity for doubt and skepticism. There will always be an attempt to explain the unexplainable, to put the Resurrection in relatable terms. But instead of arguing and trying to prove the Resurrection, we Christians are better off believing by faith and then living as those for whom the Resurrection has changed everything.

Let's be honest. We derive a certain peace from things being predictable. We believe that the state will keep us safe and keep order. Death might not be welcome, but at least it's dependable and permanent.

In an episode of the old television show *The Twilight Zone*, a traveling salesman arrives in an Old West town, offering to resurrect the town's deceased. His purported ability excites many townspeople, who long to reunite with their departed.

But at least one man is concerned. His deceased brother, whom he murdered, is in the cemetery. So he and others pay the charlatan not to resurrect the dead. In the end, the peddler leaves town with a lot of money.[9]

But on Easter Sunday, the earth quakes as we find out that everything's changed. Our old assumptions are now invalid. Our old expectations no longer hold up.

Remember when you were a child and you would sometimes make up a new game with your friends? You were the author of the rules, what could and couldn't be done. That also gave you a certain power to change the rules along the way. "It's my game. I made the rules. I can change them if I want."

The Resurrection is a striking reminder that God made the rules and God reserves the right to decide what can and can't happen. Thankfully, God has decided to set loose the Resurrection power all over creation! So the rules have changed. Death doesn't have the last word. Easter isn't just about a dead body that comes back to life. Easter is about resurrection, and resurrection changes everything.

Don't be afraid. He is risen! Go and tell!

Where is "Galilee" in your time and place? Who are you called to go and tell about the risen Jesus?

God of Life, receive my adoration and glory on this Day of Resurrection! You are alive forever! Where I am complacent, give me a holy awe. Where I am afraid, comfort me; in Jesus' name I pray. Amen.

1. From Hyde Park United Methodist Church sermon archive.
2. From *Feasting on the Gospels—Matthew: a Feasting on the Word Commentary*, by William H. Willimon. Edited by Cynthia A. Jarvis and E. Elizabeth Johnson (Louisville, Kentucky: Westminster John Knox Press, 2013); page 358.
3. From "Matthew 28:1-10," by Paul Sevier Minear in *Interpretation*, Volume 38, Number 1 (1984); page 60.
4. From "Matthew 28:1-10," by E. Carson Brisson in *Interpretation*, Volume 65, Number 1 (2011); page 74.
5. From *The New Interpreter's Bible*, Volume VIII (Nashville: Abingdon Press, 1995); page 501.
6. From *Matthew: Interpretation: A Bible Commentary for Teaching and Preaching*, by Douglas R. A. Hare (Louisville, Kentucky: Westminster John Knox Press, 2009); page 328.
7. From *Abingdon New Testament Commentaries: Matthew*, by Donald Senior (Nashville: Abingdon Press, 1998); page 343.
8. From *Feasting on the Gospels*; page 362.
9. From "Mr. Garrity and the Graves," on *The Twilight Zone*, Season 5, Episode 32, (May 8, 1964), created by Rod Serling, as cited in "Easter Fears," by P. C. Enniss Jr. in *Journal for Preachers*, Volume 11, Number 3 (1988); pages 11-12.

EASTER MONDAY
Matthew 28:1-15

If I was one of Jesus' original disciples, I would have headed for Galilee too. In 2015, I had an opportunity to visit the Holy Land. Of the three areas I visited, I was most uneasy in Jerusalem and most at peace in Galilee.

In Galilee, we took a boat out on the Sea of Galilee. I remember the steady, gentle breeze; the sound of the water lapping against our boat; the gulls flying around us, the sun warming our skin. Later, we walked through the Valley of the Wind (an area not specifically mentioned in the Bible), located west of the Sea of Galilee. I dipped my hand in a fresh water stream while also noticing cows grazing on the hillside. For lunch, we sat in an Israeli commune and had a kind of tilapia known locally as "St. Peter's fish." It was a lovely, idyllic part of the trip.

In Jerusalem, however, I was afraid to venture outside after dark. Around every corner, someone stared at me with suspicion in their eyes. Every space was divided—this was Jewish property, that was Muslim property—and tension hung in the air. When our return flight home was cancelled, I started crying and told my husband we had to get out of that town. I said to him, "I understand how Jesus got crucified here."

You know what was ironic about the stories I just told you? We were there when Israel and Syria were exchanging missile fire, and the missiles from Syria were hitting Galilee. In fact, a missile hit a day before we got there, but I felt safe there; while in Jerusalem, I felt as if there was a threat around every corner.

I am certain that the disciples felt threatened in Jerusalem. They were in danger there. Little wonder they went home! In the first place, having seen Jesus arrested and crucified, they thought the story was over. In the second place, when we are threatened, it is a natural response to go home. They returned to where they felt safe and where they felt peaceful.

And Jesus promised to meet them there! Imagine the power of that moment! Imagine how all the fear, threat, and worry they had experienced would simply disappear! Well, okay, it didn't go exactly so smoothly. They would, however, find themselves at home. They thought it was the home they knew before Jesus was there. Instead, it was home because Jesus was there.

Obviously, fear was a central emotion for the women in this passage, and surely that was the case for the disciples who fled. The resurrected Christ, however, took away all those fears. He overcomes everything we have to fear, including death. And he meets us where we need him on the road of life and makes wherever we are feel like home.

Lord Jesus, we rejoice in your resurrection, and we are thankful that you can take away all our fears. Praise the Lord, and Hallelujah! Amen.

Bible Studies to Grow Your Faith!
Learn more at AdultBibleStudies.com/LTW_Toward

IF YOU	THEN	HERE'S
# LIKE	# TRY	# WHY

Taylor W. Mills
With Gary Thompson and Michelle Morris

Toward
the
Cross

Heart-Shaping Lessons
for Lent and Easter

Comprehensive ongoing Bible studies that connect you with the Word of God and the God of the Word while suggesting engaging life-changing spiritual practices.

Thoughtful, practical daily reflections on Bible texts.

9 781791 028947